Praise for

FOUNDED

"*Founded* is the ultimate guide for accelerating your startup's progress! I wish I had this book before launching my startup, Amper—it would have set the right foundation and saved a ton of time and mistakes in going from zero to one. This book is a cheat code to making the wild adventure of building your company more intentional, fun, and focused!"

—Akshat Thirani, Garage alum, CEO and co-founder, Amper

"The advice in *Founded* is what I wish I knew before starting my first company in college. The early stages of company building can be difficult, and *Founded* does a great job of consolidating important pieces of information around customer discovery, product validation, and legal. I would highly recommend anyone even considering entrepreneurship to check it out!"

—Sarah Ahmad, Garage alum,
CEO and co-founder, Stable (YC W20)

"*Founded* is the distillation of thousands of firsthand student experiences with company building. It crystallizes those journeys into a fantastic and practical guide for the aspiring student founder."

—Manish Patel, partner, Nava Ventures, and lecturer at Stanford

FOUNDED

The No B.S. Guide for Student Entrepreneurs

MELISSA KAUFMAN
AND MIKE RAAB

AN INC.
ORIGINAL

An Inc. Original
New York, New York
www.anincoriginal.com

Distributed by River Grove Books

Design and composition by Greenleaf Book Group and Mimi Bark
Cover design by Greenleaf Book Group and Mimi Bark
Cover images used under license from ©Shutterstock.com/Brian A Jackson;
©Shutterstock.com/Stanisic Vladimir

Publisher's Cataloging-in-Publication data is available.

Print ISBN: 978-1-63909-007-5

eBook ISBN: 978-1-63909-008-2

First Edition

For our students

"Don't think of 'the Valley' as some ZIP codes in California. It is a state of mind that can be anywhere, for everyone."

—JOHN DOERR

CONTENTS

Preface

THE GARAGE

The Garage at Northwestern University was founded in 2015 and is a community and physical space for every Northwestern student interested in entrepreneurship to learn, iterate, and grow. It supports university students at all levels of study—undergraduate, graduate, and PhD. In its first six years, The Garage supported thousands of students and incubated over 1,000 student-founded startups.

At The Garage, we've learned a lot about student entrepreneurship. This unique perspective has allowed us to observe patterns for success in student founders, as well as common pitfalls and misperceptions about entrepreneurship. Our goal with this book is to help you learn from these experiences.

Growing The Garage from scratch has given us the opportunity to build what we wish we'd had as college students. We've combined real-world learnings from our professional experiences with the startup ecosystem in Silicon Valley to create the ultimate community and destination for student founders.

Although The Garage is named after the proverbial scrappy startup garage that the most valuable companies were founded in (e.g., Apple, Microsoft), our physical space is actually housed on the second floor of a parking garage. It's meant to feel raw and unfinished, despite being hyperdesigned by Gensler, one of the top architectural firms in the world, responsible for designing Facebook's headquarters and *The Washington Post*'s offices, among many others.

The space has polished cement floors and exposed ceilings. It's filled with neon signs, beanbags, dry erase walls, graffiti artwork, and every other startup cliché. We love when employees of startups or tech companies visit and tell us that it reminds them of their office. We want students to get comfortable in a work environment without assigned seats or cubicles but with perks like free snacks and robots roaming around, so they will feel more at home in these environments in the future.

More important than our physical space is the vibrant and diverse community of student entrepreneurs that has flourished at The Garage. The students are brilliant. What they lack in experience they make up for in curiosity and the willingness to try, learn, and iterate. Kellogg MBA students work alongside undergraduates, and music majors sit next to electrical engineers. The community is bonded over a desire to build their ideas, and students encourage each other to take risks. They are each other's first beta customers and share valuable knowledge and resources.

The students are also supported by a broader community of staff members, professional service providers, and volunteer mentors and experts. The staff prioritize the student experience, building relationships with the students and ensuring they get the resources they need to be successful. Vetted attorneys, accountants, and other professional service providers volunteer their time and expertise to meet with student founders during office hours. Each student team is paired with a business professional or seasoned entrepreneur who serves as a dedicated team mentor. In addition, hundreds of alums and business leaders in our expert network have offered to take calls and meetings with our student founders.

The Garage isn't a class, and there aren't any grades. Instead, it is a series of experiences designed to teach students an entrepreneurial mindset and skill set through experiential learning. We believe students learn entrepreneurship through repeat exposure to entrepreneurship, such as meeting experienced founders, visiting startup offices, collaborating with like-minded peers, and, most importantly, working on their own entrepreneurial project.

By normalizing this style of activity, students learn how to think and act like an entrepreneur. We're also proponents of the "see one, do one, teach one" philosophy. Many of our students will join another startup team their freshman year, then launch their own ventures in their sophomore and junior years, and many of them become peer mentors in their senior year, advising younger students based on their own experiences. We encourage our students to live Paul Graham's mantra of "Make something people want."

We also wrote this book because there is an overwhelming amount of bad advice and misleading information about entrepreneurship online, and much of it is from people with very little entrepreneurial experience or exposure themselves who are solely looking to profit from uninformed and vulnerable young people with an interest in entrepreneurship. Our goal is to cut through the noise and give you practical, tested advice on how to get started without any of that intimidating jargon or hustle culture. The ideas and lessons we'll discuss are based on real-world learnings and anecdotes from student founders.

Finally, we wrote this book because we deeply believe that entrepreneurship is a force for good—both in individuals' lives and in greater society. While we have the privilege of working with a few hundred student entrepreneurs each year, we knew that putting our philosophy into a book could increase the reach of these concepts, encouraging others who don't have access to the resources and community of The Garage to build something of their own.

This book is split into two parts. In the first part, we'll teach you the high-level philosophy, strategies, and frameworks for how to get started on building your venture, as well as what to expect along the way. The second part, which is based on our entry-level Tinker program at The Garage, dives more into the nitty-gritty of building a company, from evaluating ideas to business models, customer acquisition, building a team, pitching your company, and more.

You will get the most out of this book if you read through it once before you start building your idea. That way, you can internalize the lessons and philosophy and avoid some of the common mistakes many entrepreneurs make. Then, whenever you're struggling or have questions about what to do next, pick up the book and find what you need to help you navigate any particular area.

We hope this book, and the actions it inspires you to take, will have the same transformative effect on your life that The Garage has had on many of the student entrepreneurs who have passed through our garage door. The fact that you were curious and motivated enough to pick up this book is a positive sign of the potential within you to build your dreams and transform your life, and we couldn't be more humbled to help you.

Introduction

ENTREPRENEURSHIP IS A SUPERPOWER

"Life can be much broader once you discover one simple fact: Everything around you that you call life was made up by people that were no smarter than you. And you can change it; you can influence it. . . . Once you learn that, you'll never be the same again."

—**STEVE JOBS,** in an interview with the Santa Clara Valley Historical Association

Congratulations! By picking up this book, you're about to change your life forever. No, really! Being able to think and act like an entrepreneur is a superpower. And the best part is that once you embrace this mindset and learn this skill set, there's no going back.

The entrepreneurial toolkit you'll learn about in this book is about creation, taking action, and making decisions. This toolkit empowers you with agency so you can act independently, make your own choices, and make a difference in the world. Entrepreneurship allows you to work at the intersection of your passion, values, and talents. It may lead to your life's work and calling or toward a career path you wouldn't have discovered otherwise. It can open doors and manifest opportunities.

Everything we make—be it a car, an app, a painting, a social network, or a rocket ship—started as an idea and was brought to life by a person just like you. Once you realize this, you begin to see that you're more in control of this world and your own life than you ever imagined. You have the power to chart your own path, no matter how untraditional or uncommon it may be. You also have the power to shape the world around you. And you can help solve the problems facing humanity, our planet, and the future. Entrepreneurship will teach you all of this and much more.

There are lots of people in this world with great ideas. There are very few who can turn great ideas into something brand new. In this book, we're going to teach you what you need to do to become a doer and how to get started right away. What you choose to do with this superpower is up to you.

This superpower can make you smarter

There's no better way to learn something than by doing it, and as an entrepreneur, you will be doing a lot of different things. From recruiting others to managing a team, setting culture, selling a vision and product, resolving conflicts, and thinking on your feet, among other tasks, your experiences will arm you with knowledge you couldn't possibly accumulate in any other job.

This superpower can make you wealthy

Let's face it. You don't become wealthy working for someone else. Take a look at *Fortune*'s list of the richest people in the world, and you will see that they are all entrepreneurs. This skill set isn't guaranteed to make you wealthy, but you won't ever find yourself on this list without it. If you want the financial freedom to choose how you spend your time, learning how to create value in the world is the surest way to reach this goal.

This superpower can make you more attractive

Okay, not in the physical sense. But we are naturally attracted to unique individuals who forge their own paths through life, and doing so will make you more interesting. Enthusiasm is contagious. There's something magnetic about talking to someone with a passion for what they're working on. Their eyes light up, and you can feel their energy. They are excited, so you are too.

This superpower can lead to a more fulfilling life

Learning who you are, what you value, what you're good at, how you like to spend your time, and the types of people you like to be surrounded by are really important to designing a life that you find fulfilling. You can read lots of self-help books or go on a vision quest to learn some of these things, but there's no quicker path to answering each of these questions than to work on your own entrepreneurial endeavor. You'll learn what your strengths and weaknesses are, what you enjoy focusing your time and attention on the most, what your priorities are, and just how big of an impact you can have on the world around you. This self-awareness is a key ingredient to personal satisfaction and fulfillment.

This superpower will help you avoid regrets

One of the top regrets of terminally ill patients is "I wish I'd had the courage to live a life true to myself, not the one others expected of me."[1] Can you imagine anything more depressing than lying on your deathbed wondering "what if?" What if I had started that nonprofit? What if I had built a fitness company? What if I had actually put in the effort to be an artist?

Finding the courage to take the proverbial leap is difficult. But the good news is it gets easier and easier each time, because you receive the benefits of being true to yourself and realize that you really have nothing to lose.

---

1   Ware, B. (2011). *The Top Five Regrets of the Dying: A Life Transformed by the Dearly Departing*. Hay House Inc.

When there's enough passion and conviction to act, you will leap. And if you decide not to, it won't be because of fear or lack of knowledge but, rather, because you decided not to. You will be in control of your choices and your destiny, and you'll never have to wonder, "What if I would have . . . ?"

There's a lot we won't cover in this book. This book *is not* foolproof advice that will make it impossible for you to fail. This is not a step-by-step "how to" guide for building a billion-dollar tech unicorn. This is not an instruction booklet for how to scale a company to millions of customers. This book also won't get into the legal nuances of founding a company. And it is certainly not a memoir or biography about our experiences founding a company.

Instead, this book is a reference for first-time founders, with a focus on student founders, although the information is relevant for all founders. The pages ahead offer inspiration and an honest look at what it takes to bring your idea from inception to fruition. We'll discuss our philosophy about entrepreneurship, provide some useful frameworks for you to utilize, and give you some concrete steps to help you get started on your next idea. We'll also share what we've learned from observing and guiding successful founders, as well as common misperceptions and mistakes in hopes that you can avoid them. You'll learn why, regardless of the eventual success or failure of any individual venture, you should take the plunge into entrepreneurship. We've made it simple so you can take those first strides. But at the end of the day, *you* are going to need to take action if you want the information in this book to be useful.

College or graduate school is a great time to work on an entrepreneurial endeavor. Unburdened by the responsibilities you will shoulder later in life and at the peak of your creative and intellectual capabilities, you're prepared and more willing to try something totally new. Universities are a hotbed of intelligent, interesting people with a diversity of skill sets and life experiences. There will never be a time in your life when you are surrounded by so many smart people from different backgrounds and world-class experts in a variety of fields. In fact, the best entrepreneurial teams are founded by diverse teams with complementary values and skill sets. Chances are, the skill set or expertise you need is somewhere in your university, and your job as an entrepreneur is to find those people and convince them to join you.

Furthermore, as entrepreneurship has gone from being trendy on college campuses to a critical resource to attract the smartest students, many campuses are flush with resources to support you. Many of these resources are only available while you're a student, so you should take advantage of them while you have unlimited access to them. The goal of many university incubators is to expose students to an entrepreneurial mindset to teach you what it actually means to hustle, pitch, and lead effective teams.

The biggest downside you will face working on an entrepreneurial project during school is balancing your entrepreneurial project with the rest of your life: classes, work, friends, and activities. Creating something new takes a tremendous amount of time and effort. This is why it is really important that you work on something that is authentic to you. But guess what? At any point in your life, you'll need to balance competing priorities and domains. As a student, chances are you have fewer serious life commitments than you will later in life and have very little to lose if your startup doesn't succeed. And best of all, you have so much to gain.

Regardless of whether your venture is successful, building something of your own is one of the most empowering things you can do for your career and your life. By doing so, your project becomes an authentic expression of who you are. This authenticity is critical for your venture to succeed, but even if your venture fails, living authentically attracts new opportunities, puts you in places you might not have been in otherwise, and gives you a dynamic story to tell.

IT ISN'T SUPPOSED TO BE EASY

While we're big believers in the power and benefits of entrepreneurship, we're also believers in being up front and straightforward, so we aren't going to tell you this is going to be easy. That's because building something new that others value is incredibly time consuming and difficult. And that's okay. If it were easy, everyone would do it!

You've taken the first step by picking up this book. But just reading it (or any other resources) will not make you a successful entrepreneur. You have to do the work, put in the effort, and persevere through all of the adversity along the way.

As the fictional astronaut hero Mark Watney from the blockbuster film *The Martian* put it, "At some point, everything is going to go south on you, and you're going to say 'This is it. This is how [it ends].' Now you can either accept that, or you can get to work. That's all there is to it. You just begin. You do the math. You solve one problem. And then you solve the next problem and the next problem. And if you solve enough problems, you get to come home."

Luckily for you, the stakes are much lower than surviving on a deserted planet, but the concepts remain true for entrepreneurs: Get to work. Do the math. Solve the problem. Find your first ten customers, then the next hundred, and then the next thousand. If you solve enough problems and find enough customers, you get to chart your own path in life.

Although it won't be easy and success is not guaranteed, no matter the outcome of any individual project or startup, you'll be glad you gave it a shot. When students at The Garage shutter a project they've been working on—sometimes for years—we ask them if they regretted working on the project or wished that they hadn't tried it. The answer is always the same: No regrets. The knowledge learned, experiences gained, and relationships forged were so valuable that they wouldn't undo them, even knowing that the project wouldn't succeed. More importantly, they've learned valuable lessons, have gained confidence in their abilities, and are even better prepared for their next entrepreneurial journey.

Part I

DISCOVERING YOUR SUPERPOWER

(1)

ENTREPRENEURSHIP IS FOR EVERYONE

We read and hear an outsized amount about Silicon Valley startups and founders. These companies are usually technology companies and are often backed by venture capital. In reality, 16% of the US adult population are entrepreneurs, but only 0.62% of startups raise venture capital funding.[2] This has warped many students' perceptions of what entrepreneurship is. You don't need to raise venture capital or build a company valued at a billion dollars to be an entrepreneur. Similarly, you don't need millions of dollars to start a business: The foodie who starts her

---

2 Madden, D. (2018). "Is It Time to Raise VC Funding? Ask Yourself These 4 Questions to Find Out." *Inc.* https://www.inc.com/debbie-madden/4-reasons-you-dont-need-vc-money-for-your-startup.html

own restaurant is an entrepreneur, the writer with a paid newsletter is an entrepreneur, and the professional taking wedding photos on the weekends is an entrepreneur.

At The Garage, our definition of entrepreneurship is quite broad. We think of it as the process of bringing any new idea to life. Some people think of entrepreneurship as starting a business, like a coffee shop, or building a big tech company, like Snapchat. We like to include all new ideas from starting a podcast to creating a musical ensemble to designing and selling a new style of notebook. Entrepreneurship is about starting anything! Entrepreneurial ideas can be for-profit, not-for-profit, or arts-based projects. In all cases, they require a product, experience, or service that is consumed by users, customers, or an audience. Your product or service should create value that someone is willing to pay for in some way, whether it's a customer, an advertiser, a subscriber, a donor, or another business.

We also borrow the definition of entrepreneurship from Australian entrepreneur Sam Prince that entrepreneurship is an activity and not an identity. It's something you do, not who you are. There are many types of entrepreneurs. Some people do entrepreneurial things on nights and weekends after their day job. Others add entrepreneurial "chapters" to their careers, oscillating between starting companies and working for companies, while others become serial entrepreneurs and hop from venture to venture with brief breaks along the away.

We believe that entrepreneurship is for everyone! It's not an innate talent, which means anyone can learn to be an entrepreneur.

Learning how entrepreneurs think and act will serve you well whether you go on to become a serial entrepreneur or a doctor, lawyer, business executive, artist, environmentalist, caregiver, musician, designer, parent, or any other path you may choose. The skills you learn—like collaborating, prioritizing, listening, adapting, and taking risks—are applicable to everyone.

Throughout this book, we'll occasionally jump into an anecdote from a student who has passed through The Garage that emphasizes the value of the concept we're talking about. We think these real-life stories demonstrate *how* and *why* these frameworks are useful, and we hope they aren't too jarring.

Here's the first one: Growing up in Kansas City, Missouri, Lauren Washington never thought of herself as a businessperson, and she certainly didn't think of herself as an entrepreneur. During her junior year of high school, she took a film photography class and an English class and fell in love with film and creative writing. She also began to delve into other creative arts, including photography, attending the NAACP convention, and taking photos to build her first online portfolio. During her senior year of high school, she got her first taste of screenwriting and produced her own mini documentary titled *The Importance of Representation in the Entertainment Industry*.

Her older, more entrepreneurial brother, Brandon, on the other hand, started a music label in middle school, recruiting musicians and building an audience of 3,000 subscribers on YouTube. In high school, Lauren helped Brandon expand the idea to include visual artists, fashion designers, and other creatives like herself. They named this community of artists FILO.

In college, Lauren majored in film. Her eyes were opened after a school-organized trip to Los Angeles to explore the film industry, visiting companies like Hulu and FX. That trip solidified her focus on screenwriting and directing, and it also helped her realize she wanted to be in charge of her own unique career path and that she didn't want a traditional job.

Intrigued by this idea of independence, Lauren took an introductory entrepreneurship class, and it changed her thinking completely. Through that class and the programming at The Garage, Lauren realized "artists are inherently entrepreneurs, because they make new ideas and put them out in the world . . . and I realized that I was a creative entrepreneur."

Today, Lauren and Brandon are still working together on FILO and running it as a startup. They are launching a platform for creative artists and partnering with brands to offer unique opportunities for their community—for example, partnering with visual artists to produce posters and other visuals for film projects.

Lauren plans to pursue a career as a film director, but, through her startup, she has learned important skills that she believes will make her a better, more creative film professional. She has learned the importance of being comfortable with ambiguity, pivoting ideas, finding other people to join her vision, patience, networking, and advocating for herself and her ideas. She advises other students, "If you want to create something for yourself, take a step away from what you think entrepreneurship is. It's really for anyone who wants to create new ideas, and it has value no matter what career path you take."

While we couldn't agree more, entrepreneurship is not for everyone. "But wait, I thought you just said . . . ?" Yes, but hear us out. While the skill set and mindset are for everyone, being a founder isn't. In recent years, the media has glamorized being a founder through movies like *The Social Network* and television shows like HBO's *Silicon Valley*. In reality, being a full-time entrepreneur is for very few people. As a career, it is a very non-traditional path and one that can be lonely, frustrating, and full of uncertainty. It's very different and much more difficult than showing up at a job and having a boss tell you what to do every day. Some people don't like the ambiguity, the challenge, and the whiplash from the high highs and low lows. It's completely okay to prefer a job and lifestyle with a steady paycheck and less responsibility.

Our broad definition of entrepreneurship is inclusive of everyone working on an idea for something new that doesn't exist in the world today. The process of learning to be an entrepreneur can fundamentally change your life and unlock opportunities most people can only dream of. During this process, you will meet incredible people, develop yourself as a leader, and gain a better understanding of the world around you.

Success in entrepreneurship is not binary. We believe the lessons you will learn from an entrepreneurial pursuit are applicable no matter what you do professionally. An entrepreneurial skill set is critical for an entrepreneur, but it is equally important for anyone who wants to lead and make change in any field or industry. Before we dive in, we'll tell you a little more about our philosophy and why, regardless of whether your entrepreneurial project is a success or a failure, it'll make you a better, more well-rounded person.

KEY TAKEAWAYS

- We define entrepreneurship broadly as the process of bringing any new idea to life.

- Entrepreneurship is an activity, not an identity; it's something you do, not who you are.

- Entrepreneurship is for everyone, and the mindset and skill set you learn are applicable to all career paths.

(2)

FORGING YOUR OWN PATH

One of the lessons that many first-time founders unfortunately learn too late is that it's imperative to set the values and culture of an organization early on and that being intentional and focused can pay dividends in the future. In this chapter, we'll explore the values and philosophy that we've chosen to help our student entrepreneurs at The Garage.

TRUST YOURSELF

We believe in the potential of your ideas. Each of us occupies a unique set of life experiences and perspectives that allows us to see problems or opportunities in different ways. This is true even when you are a young student and don't yet have a lot of professional experience. Look around your campus, your community, and the world. What problems or opportunities do you see? What excites you?

Many students feel they don't have the right skills to start something. This isn't true. The internet empowers you to learn almost any skill, to connect with people interested in what you're working on, and to reach a large, engaged audience.

For example, Mateo Price first came to The Garage with a friend and was interested in learning more about startups. In high school, as a passionate sports fan, he cofounded a sports blog and grew it from 20,000 to 5 million page views. Developing an online advertising strategy and managing the demands of a writing staff proved too much for a group of mostly sixteen-year-olds, and the site's traffic began a slow, lethal decline over the next year. In college, he majored in economics and psychology and continued to explore his passion for digital marketing and branding.

Ready for his next entrepreneurial project, Mateo came to Melissa's office, and she asked him what he was interested in. He said he'd been following a sports influencer on YouTube named Jesse (@jesser). Melissa encouraged Mateo to reach out to Jesse to offer to help him with his marketing. A few months later, after telling Jesse via email that he "was going to be in LA," Mateo booked a flight to Los Angeles to meet with Jesse. After spending the day together, Jesse hired Mateo to optimize his YouTube presence.

Two years later, that first project has grown into Authentic Media Ascension (AMA), a growth analytics and digital strategy company that has helped YouTube influencers earn an extra $5 million dollars. Mateo and his team at AMA have brought in hundreds of thousands of dollars in revenue, all while still full-time college students. Not bad for a student, right?

Mateo didn't learn about YouTube analytics and strategy in class. Just like when he learned to grow his high school sports blog, he trusted himself to work hard to create the experiences and opportunities that excited him most. This has led to a journey full of enthusiasm and learning.

Chances are, the more you look, the more you'll see challenges and opportunities that you have the power to address. Which challenges are you most motivated to solve? Which challenge or opportunity do you connect with most deeply? Which challenges or opportunities align most closely with your talents and interests?

Trust yourself to have great ideas and to figure things out. Your unique perspective, knowledge, skills, and drive give you the power to forge new ideas and change the world!

DO THE WORK

A lot of people want to "be an entrepreneur," but few are willing to put in the work. You'll often see this when someone excitedly tells you about their ideas but never seems to actually make them a reality. To learn to be an entrepreneur, you must be an entrepreneur, which means doing the thing. Remember, being an entrepreneur is an activity. You can read books, articles, and case studies about famous founders and their companies, but to learn how entrepreneurs think and act, you must start your own project and do the work.

Starting a business or venture requires work—and a lot of it. Some students think that updating their LinkedIn to say "founder" makes them an entrepreneur, but breathing life into a new idea requires a lot more effort. You will be managing sales calls, team disputes, funding scarcity, product development, engaging with mentors, and a million other things at the same time.

Long hours, late nights, and constantly thinking about and working on your venture are all required. Some of the work feels glamorous, like speaking to the press or hopping on an airplane to pitch a big customer. However, a lot of the work is monotonous, like sending cold emails, diving into analytics dashboards, and reconciling your business bank account. In a startup, even the CEO takes out the trash.

If you want to develop big muscles, you've got to put in a lot of reps. Similarly, if you want to develop yourself as an entrepreneur, you need to get in a lot of reps. Each time you pitch your idea, each time you interview a potential user, each time you solve a problem you're facing, you're getting in a rep. And with each rep, you get a little smarter and faster for the next one.

Ibraheem Alinur worked on five entrepreneurial projects as a student at Northwestern. He got his reps in working for other students' startups before launching his own company. He ran marketing for a tutoring business and growth for a platform for discovering new opportunities on college campuses. He conducted hundreds of user interviews and recruited early new customers. At one point, he was even helping build a tabletop dishwasher.

As an industrial engineering major and entrepreneurship minor, Ibraheem had a talent for seeing the big picture and structuring organizations around new ideas. His junior year, he cofounded City Health Tech, a company building the future of disease prevention solutions. Their first product, Opal, is a device that sits next to sinks and encourages hand washing.

Ibraheem recently raised his initial seed funding after an arduous monthslong process. He shared, "I heard 'no' 73 times before I finally heard 'yes.' I knew that each time I pitched an investor, I was getting a rep in and getting better and better at telling my story."

Building a new idea requires hard work. Don't get stuck in thinking or planning mode. Instead, focus on doing. Make a move, gather feedback, make another move. The best way to learn and improve is to roll up your sleeves and do the work over and over again.

FORGE YOUR OWN PATH

One of the most exciting parts of working on an entrepreneurial project is that you have no idea where it may lead. It may be hard to put yourself out there, try something new, and accept that you might fail or might not reap rewards immediately, but because your project is an authentic expression of yourself and you're committed to it, you often find opportunities and experiences that you may not have discovered otherwise.

Rachel Cantor studied communications and French at Northwestern. In high school, she launched an online news source for teens, written by teens from all over the globe. Since then, she has had an interest in entrepreneurship and startups. During college, Rachel took entrepreneurship classes and helped several student-founded startups at The Garage with their marketing. Her entrepreneurial spirit and go-getter mentality were recognized by faculty and staff. And as a sophomore, she was selected for a fellowship program for undergraduate students with high entrepreneurial potential.

Rachel took on several leadership roles within a student-run marketing agency, and during her senior year, she served as the executive cochair for Northwestern University's Dance Marathon, one of the largest student-run philanthropies in the nation. It was through leading student organizations that she flexed her entrepreneurial mindset.

In the spring of her senior year, Rachel decided to start a personal recommendations newsletter. For as long as she can remember, Rachel has always been that go-to friend when it comes to podcast, TV, book, and product recommendations, and she thought a newsletter would be a fun way to share her tips, suggestions, and experiences as a new grad.

Her newsletter was the perfect culmination of her interest in entrepreneurship, her talent for writing, and her passion for marketing. It quickly gained hundreds of followers and attracted the founders of a sustainable startup called Brightly, a new discovery platform that combines content, community, and shopping to ignite change for conscious consumers. Rachel further explored her love for writing and building brands as a freelance writer for Brightly, where she wrote their weekly newsletter. She grew its subscribers and helped the team use the newsletter as a new revenue stream.

While freelancing, Rachel continued to write her personal newsletter every week. In one newsletter, she included a piece of content from the media company Morning Brew. On a whim, Rachel tweeted a link to her newsletter and tagged Morning Brew, not really thinking that it would result in anything. A few hours later, she received the following message from one of the managing editors at Morning Brew:

> I read your newsletter for the first time today since you tagged Morning Brew in a tweet, and I loved it. You clearly love to read a "shit ton of content" and curate it for people. Not sure if you are aware, but we're hiring a full-time writer to lead what we're calling (for now) our Brew Recs vertical . . . Let me know if you are interested in applying!

Today, Rachel is responsible for writing Morning Brew's latest newsletter, *Sidekick*, which has over 170,000 readers. She didn't start her newsletter with the intention of getting a job at Morning Brew. She started it because it aligned with her interests, skills, and passions. If she hadn't taken the risk and put her writing and unique perspective out there in the world, she probably would not have found and landed her role at Morning Brew. Being true to yourself gives you the courage to forge your own unique path and career. Who knows? Your next idea could launch the career of your dreams.

CELEBRATE FAILURE

We're going to be honest with you. Although we understand that every founder obviously wants their idea to succeed, the tough reality is that most ideas will fail. The most valuable lesson, regardless of success or failure, is what you learn about yourself, your industry, and your project along the way. We want to rid you of the notion that failure is something to be afraid of or that you shouldn't act on it because your idea might not be successful.

If you're going to be an entrepreneur, failure is inevitable. Many people's immediate reaction to failure is to hide it, ignore it, or be ashamed and embarrassed by it. Most of our reactions to failure end up being counterproductive and a complete waste of time.

At The Garage, we encourage students to celebrate failure. We've tried to build this into the culture by asking students to share a recent failure and what they learned from it in front of their peers at our weekly dinner. We memorialize the failure by having the student pop a confetti popper. While, early in the school year, there are very few students willing to volunteer to tell a room of their peers how they failed that week, they quickly learn there is nothing to fear. It often feels like lifting a weight off their shoulders when they realize there's no need to hide or feel ashamed of things that didn't work out and that the community is supportive of them regardless.

As a founder, you're going to get rejected, turned down, and passed on thousands of times. This is an inescapable fact, even if your company turns out to be wildly successful. Most people don't like change or challenges to the status quo. When a founder presents a new idea even to friends and family, they will often be told that their idea is ridiculous, frivolous, or just downright terrible.

Think about it. Before Uber and Lyft, the idea of summoning a ride on your phone and getting into a stranger's car was unimaginable. This idea seemed pretty crazy and "out there," but founders must be visionaries and imagine the world the way they want it to be, not the way it is. If you're afraid of being turned down, you're unlikely to ask for the things you want and need to make your company succeed.

Ironically, the best way to improve your reaction to failure is to fail, which helps build your immunity to it. The more times we experience failure, the more numb we become to the sting of it. Maybe the first time we take a big swing publicly and miss, we feel a lot of shame and embarrassment. But after a bit of time, we realize that we're actually okay and that we learned something from the attempt that we otherwise wouldn't have.

As Lucas Philips, the founder of Brewbike, stated in our podcast, *How I Got Here*, "You can fail and be okay. You'll just go back to your dorm room and go to class the next day. And yeah, maybe there will be some embarrassment or something like that, but that will pass. People will honestly respect you for doing this thing. And you'll learn so much in the process. And so, there's no better way I think to learn to be an entrepreneur than actually just doing the thing."

Building resiliency is the antidote to failure and is a key skill and trait of successful founders. As a founder, you'll hear "no" from customers, people you want to hire, investors, and many more. This may lead you to second-guess yourself. You'll have to use your own common sense to determine when to listen to this feedback and when to ignore it. Learning how to ask for what you want, overcoming rejection, and becoming immune to hearing "no" is empowering. So start practicing. Ask a customer if they will buy your product. Ask your boss for a raise. Ask your dry cleaner for a discount. Regardless of what it is, you're putting yourself out there and building your resilience.

The first time you get turned down is very difficult. By the 1,000th time you're rejected, however, you're already moving on to the next ask. At The Garage, we've done daylong exercises with students—inspired by Jia Jiang's Ted Talk titled "100 Days of Rejection"—to help them build their resiliency by asking for ridiculous things. For example, we'd have them ask to have a burger refill at their favorite fast-food restaurant or ask if they could pick flowers from someone's garden or ask if they could work for an hour at their favorite bookstore.

During this exercise, we ask students to take photos along the way to document their day. You'd be shocked by how often the answer is "yes," and we get a photo of a student spending an hour shelving books or picking flowers, although we've never had a student successfully get a burger refill . . . yet.

Russell Marriott joined NoteShark, an online marketplace where students could buy and sell notes for their classes, his junior year at Northwestern as the marketing manager. The cofounders, who were also Northwestern undergraduates, thought NoteShark would create a more collaborative environment by sharing materials for classes. The idea was to use money as an incentive for students to share their class notes with other students who either missed a class or wanted to supplement their own notes. The team was excited about their idea and thought their venture would revolutionize learning on campus. But, a year later, they suspended operations.

NoteShark had a successful launch. Their website stated in big letters "Stop wasting time on verbose readings," encouraging students to use their study guides rather than complete the readings for classes. It caught the attention of the student body, and within the first twenty-four hours of launching their website, over forty students created accounts.

However, the faculty were also taking note (pun intended) and were not happy. The NoteShark team underestimated the backlash they would receive from professors, who didn't want classroom notes to be traded in the marketplace. Russell received numerous emails from professors asking that NoteShark remove notes for their classes from the website. Even though the team had consulted with intellectual property attorneys before their launch, members of the faculty claimed that NoteShark was violating their intellectual property rights. The pressure from the administration continued, and ultimately, Russell and the team shut down operations.

"Even though we failed as a business, my year with NoteShark was still an incredible experience," Russell said. In fact, at The Garage, failures are embraced alongside successes. Russell shared the NoteShark story in front of a room full of his peers. As is our tradition at The Garage, Russell popped a confetti party popper to celebrate the failure, helping his peers learn to not be afraid of failure but, rather, to embrace it and learn from it.

The silver lining to Russell's experience appeared while he was interviewing for summer internships. His final interview question for a summer internship at IBM was *What has been your biggest failure, and what have you learned from it?* Russell says, "Rather than talking about doing poorly in a class, I talked about NoteShark and our failures as a company." Russell was given a verbal offer for the internship on the spot!

Russell's experience demonstrates that the failure of a project is not the failure of a person. As the saying goes, "You learn more in defeat than in victory." Learning from your experiences, both successes and failures, is a valuable skill in entrepreneurship and in landing a job working for someone else.

KEY TAKEAWAYS

- Trust yourself. Your unique perspective, knowledge, skills, and drive give you the power to forge new ideas and change the world.

- Do the work. Building a new idea requires hard work. Don't get stuck in thinking or planning mode. Instead, make *doing* a priority.

- Forge your own path. Working on an entrepreneurial project will help you find opportunities and experiences that you may not have discovered otherwise.

- Celebrate failure. Failure is an inevitable part of an entrepreneurial journey. Each failure is a learning opportunity. Embrace it, and learn from it.

(3)

THE WARM-UP LAP

The old adage "Ideas are a dime a dozen" couldn't be more true. The world is full of incredible ideas. The internet is overflowing with lists of ideas, and we're sure you have friends and family members with ideas too. But ideas are simply that—ideas. And ideas are useless without a passionate visionary to implement them and bring them to life. That's where you come in! From here on out, it all comes down to execution. In this chapter, we'll discuss the first actionable steps you should take when you have an idea you'd like to get started on, which we refer to as the Warm-Up Lap.

In the beginning of this book, we told you there are lots of people in this world with ideas, some of which may even be really good ideas, but there are very few people who can turn an idea into something real. Why do so few people take that first step to turn their great ideas into reality?

Well, it's a scary thing. When an idea is in our head, it's safe and protected. We can dream about it and expand on it and think about all of the potential it has, how big it can grow, the impact it will have, and how great our lives will be once we build it. But the second we tell someone else about an idea or talk to potential customers or build a first version of our idea, it's suddenly incredibly vulnerable to feedback, and we may realize that our precious idea might not work. That dream life that our imagination cultivated about our inevitable success and impact is suddenly challenged.

So, many people prefer to keep their ideas in the safety of their own head, where they can continue to daydream, instead of finding out that their idea isn't perfect. We see dozens of students in our office hours at The Garage who pitch us their idea, and after we give them advice on how to get started, they disappear. The reason for this is they enjoy coming up with the ideas but fall short on the execution side of things. If you want to succeed, don't be an idea person. Be a doer. One of the first obstacles you will face is the challenge of getting started, which, again, can be a scary thing! Not to worry. We're going to show you how to get over this first hurdle.

Like any difficult journey, the first step is often the hardest. Many student founders will have a great idea and get stuck in the ideation phase. They'll want to do more research or write more code or overthink the idea. Remember, entrepreneurship is an activity. It requires action. This doesn't mean you shouldn't do research. You absolutely should. But you should have a bias toward action. Like a scientist with a hypothesis, your goal is to make assumptions and then get out there and test them.

We recommend taking a week to work through the Warm-Up Lap. This exercise requires four steps: doing light research, making something concrete related to your idea, telling someone else about what you made, and knowing why you want to do it. Often, this will invigorate you and get you more excited about the scope and potential of your idea. And sometimes, it has the opposite effect. By getting some initial feedback, you soon realize your idea might not be as tenable as you thought. While this may sound discouraging, it's better to find this out sooner rather than later. This is why the Warm-Up Lap is an important first exercise, and it only involves four steps!

STEP 1: DO SOME LIGHT RESEARCH

The first step of the Warm-Up Lap is to conduct some light research to determine the feasibility of your idea and if there's anything similar to it already available in the world. Do not spend more than a few hours on this. Typically, this step will either increase your excitement and motivation to pursue your idea or make you realize that it might not be possible due to a number of factors, including cost, regulation, or physics. You may also discover that your idea already exists and that users love it.

You'd be surprised how often we have an excited student pitch us what they believe is a brand-new product or idea, only to have a quick Google search reveal dozens of companies working on something identical. Finding competitors doesn't mean your idea is bad or wrong. In fact, sometimes it can show that you're onto something!

Research isn't limited to conducting internet searches, though. You'll also benefit from input from the types of people your startup may eventually try to work with. Make it a priority to learn from their experience and perspective. At this stage, their feedback will likely reveal problems or issues that you wouldn't have thought of on your own. Gaining this feedback before you begin to build will save you valuable time and countless mistakes.

For example, let's say your idea is a solution for restaurants that lets in-house diners order and pay from their phones, instead of through a waiter. The best initial research you could conduct would be talking to local restaurant owners to understand why they would or would not be interested in this product. You may hear that some owners think of their friendly waitstaff as a valuable part of their dining experience or that you'd need to integrate your software with their point-of-service software. Or you may find an experimental restaurateur who is excited by the idea and may volunteer to be your first customer if you build the product.

You'll find it helpful to document your learnings. Simply add to this document any time you learn something from a conversation or find a relevant article, link, or industry fact. Over time, this document will help you see the evolution of your understanding of the space you're in. You'll be able to make insights at the intersections of your learnings. Maybe you'll learn about someone who attempted a similar idea in the past or discover a way to make your idea better based on an industry trend.

A famous example of initial light research to determine the feasibility of an idea is the story of Netflix. Cofounders Reed Hastings and Marc Randolph were brainstorming startup ideas while commuting to work together. DVDs were just coming to market, replacing the much heavier and bulkier VHS tapes, and suddenly, they had the idea for an internet movie rental service.

Before they went any further with developing the idea, they chose to see if it was even feasible by buying a CD (the nearest store didn't sell DVDs yet) and mailing it to Reed's house. The next day, the CD arrived undamaged, proving they could mail DVDs for the price of a postage stamp. Imagine instead if they had spent months building a business plan before testing if mailing a DVD was even possible, only to find out that the DVDs broke in the mail. Wasted time! The first step of the Warm-Up Lap will arm you with more knowledge and information to help you avoid costly mistakes down the road like broken DVDs or creating an identical product or service that is already in the marketplace.

STEP 2: GET THE IDEA OUT OF YOUR HEAD

The second step of the Warm-Up Lap is to do something concrete to get the idea out of your head. Most of the time, the idea in your head is more glorious than what you can draw, build, explain, or market. Fear not. The goal of this step is not high-fidelity, high-quality output; rather, it is getting your idea into a form that you can share with someone you trust. Some ideas include writing a summary of your idea, making wireframes for an app or website, or creating a pitch deck. For a physical product, this may include making a conceptual drawing of your product or printing a low-fidelity 3D model.

During this step, lean into your strengths. If you are more of a visual person or designer, try making a mock-up. If you're more of a linear, analytical thinker, try writing your thoughts in a blog post. If you're a software engineer, write some code. This step should be fun!

Now would also be a good time to explore the demographic for this product or service. Is there a paying customer? If it's a consumer, try to create a persona. How old are they? Where do they live? What do they enjoy doing? Be as specific as you can. Similarly, if it's for a business, ask yourself, *What type of company might be interested? Which industry are they in? Who at the company would make the purchasing decision?*

You probably won't get this right the first time, but it's a thought exercise to anchor you. You can imagine how a wellness product for twenty-something male bodybuilders in Los Angeles might be different from a similar product for forty-something women yoginis in Berlin. This step will help ground you and give you another assumption to test and prove, as well as hone your initial focus.

STEP 3: SHOW SOMEONE ELSE

This leads us to the third step of the Warm-Up Lap: Show someone else what you created in step 2. This initial feedback could come from someone you trust, like a friend, professor, mentor, or family member, or it could be someone who may have a perspective or experience relevant to your idea. The ideal person should be someone willing to ask you questions and bring up things you might not be thinking about already. Be sure to get excited! This is your first pitch!

While you may secretly hope this person tells you this is the best idea they've ever heard, this is both unlikely and not the goal of this exercise. Instead, your goal is to get an outside perspective that can provide feedback, input, and questions that you, as an individual, have not thought of by yourself. The most important thing to communicate is the problem you're trying to solve and what you think the solution may be. The more enthusiastic you are about the problem, the better the chance the person you're talking to will get excited too. It's important to ask open-ended questions about their reaction and to take notes.

This meeting is framed as an opportunity to get some feedback on your idea. But it's also your first opportunity to practice telling your story, conveying your enthusiasm, and working on your pitch. After the meeting, ask yourself—

- Did I explain the idea concisely?
- Did I do a good job explaining the problem and solution?
- What did they disagree with or have trouble understanding?
- Was I able to incorporate any of my research into demonstrating my knowledge of this space?
- Which clarifying questions did the listener ask?
- Which of my assumptions did they disagree with?

Hopefully, the listener gave you some interesting insights or much-needed encouragement. You should have also learned a little about how the listener responded to your idea. This is a great time to reflect and look for opportunities to improve how you communicate your idea and solution.

STEP 4: KNOW YOUR WHY

Now that you have done some light research, made your idea more concrete, and solicited feedback from someone else about your project, it is a great time to ask yourself, "Am I doing this for the right reasons?" Sometimes, after you've done a little research or talked about an idea, your initial excitement will fade, or you'll come across significant roadblocks, like finding out that your online betting app is illegal or deciding that you don't want to spend all day thinking about chemical cremation (both are real examples from The Garage).

There's no doubt that part of the reason you picked up this book is because *founder* or *entrepreneur* is an alluring title to you. Some people, what we call *wantrepreneurs*, will chase any idea they think might have an inkling of a chance at success, whether or not they're actually interested in and passionate about the project. Ironically, these startups almost never succeed, because the founder was never interested in the project, solution, or problem itself, just the benefits of calling themselves a founder. Some of the most common misguided reasons people start companies are—

- They focus solely on how it will make them rich, famous, and influential.

- They want to build a social media following and believe appearing as a founder gives them clout and influence.
- The industry is "trendy," "hot," and getting lots of capital investment.

Notice that none of these common reasons for starting a company have anything to do with the actual problem that the startup is presumably solving or the ingeniousness and utility of the product. Instead, these reasons are focused on the individual's ego and the ease of garnering attention and funding. While the charade may last for a little while, your competitors, who are obsessed with their customers and their product, will eventually put you out of business.

It's also possible to start with an idea that you are passionate about but to lose interest or fall out of love with what the project becomes. This is okay! It's better to move on or close the business than to toil away on something you're not excited about or have little conviction in.

Lucas Pasch cofounded FanHome while earning his MBA. Lucas was an avid Packers fan and wanted a way to meet like-minded fans to watch games with in Chicago. The idea, modeled off of Airbnb, was that FanHome would be a platform to connect fans for in-home viewing parties.

The concept was attracting users, but not the kind that Lucas anticipated. Instead of sports enthusiasts, the platform was taking off with avid fans of the TV show *The Bachelor*. Concerned that *The Bachelor* audience was too niche, Lucas pivoted the concept again. The new idea was to bring the sports bar experience to esports.

Lucas began selling tickets to esports viewing parties at local bars. The pitch was that, rather than stream content on Twitch alone at home, enthusiasts could gather and watch live events streamed from all over the world. Similarly, it was a great way for bars to monetize what would have otherwise been a quiet midweek afternoon or evening. The idea was also compelling because, unlike traditional sports, esports didn't have an off-season.

At the time, esports had an audience of 500 million viewers, but unfortunately, Lucas wasn't one of them. After a few months of hosting parties for fans of games like Overwatch and Counter-Strike, winning a pitch competition, and attracting the attention of several investors, Lucas shuttered the company. He said, "I loved the idea of FanHome when it was about sports, but I lost my enthusiasm for the idea as it pivoted to new industries and audiences."

Lucas realized that building a company was a yearslong process, and, ultimately, he was not motivated and excited to build a product that he wasn't actually interested in or passionate about, even if it had potential to grow.

Some of you may be thinking that if fame, fortune, influence, and ego are the wrong reasons to start a company, what are the "right" reasons? This is a deeply personal question, and it boils down to who you are as an individual. Try asking yourself things like *What problems do you see in the world, and which are you passionate about solving? What subjects do you enjoy discussing with others? What do you spend your time doing? What are you obsessed with?*

If you're going to bring a new idea to life, it should be one you are deeply committed to. The word for this is *conviction*. Conviction is impossible to fake. It's also the secret ingredient to making you more convincing. You must believe in what you are doing and selling. So, take the time to convince yourself that the problem you are solving is worthy of your precious time and effort.

Entrepreneurship will test your limits, and it'll feel like an uphill battle unless you have a deep connection to the problem you're solving. You need the ability to tap deep into an inner well for inspiration and motivation. If you don't have that, you are very likely to give up when the going gets tough. You need to be driven by a deeper sense of purpose to persevere. The best entrepreneurs work at the intersection of their passion, values, and talent. They then align this with solving a real problem that someone will pay for.

The most impactful companies have been clear in their mission and vision from the start. Of course, these may shift and evolve throughout the life of the company, but if the sole mission is to make the founder rich, you have a difficult road ahead. What you'll soon learn is that one of the primary jobs of an entrepreneur is to sell. This may range from selling your product to customers to recruiting team members (and, potentially, investors) who believe in your vision and want to join the ride. It is much easier to do all of these things if you're genuinely building your company for the right reasons and the mission and vision are aligned and visible to everyone.

If you've made it this far, and you're still excited about your idea, you're ready to move on. Telling one other trusted person about your idea was a good warm-up for what comes next.

KEY TAKEAWAYS

- When you have an idea, test it out with a Warm-Up Lap:
  - Do some light research to see if your solution is feasible or already exists.
  - Get your idea out of your head and onto an external format.
  - Tell someone else and listen to their feedback.
  - Do a gut check to make sure you're the right person for the job and you're in it for the right reasons.

(4)

THINK LIKE
A SCIENTIST

After completing your Warm-Up Lap, it's important you have accurate expectations for the next part of your entrepreneurial journey. In this chapter, we'll discuss how to build a minimum viable product, get feedback, set goals, iterate, and, most importantly, cultivate the entrepreneurial skill of thinking like a scientist.

If there's one thing you take away from this book, we hope it's the belief in the process of getting your idea or product in front of others so you can gather feedback, improve your product or service, and repeat the process. We are also big fans of the scientific method! As an entrepreneur, you have an idea (theory), you build what you believe your customers want (hypothesis), and you launch a version of this product to test your hypothesis or assumptions (experiment). Your product launch and customer interviews may prove that your hypothesis was correct and that customers love your product! More likely (at least early on), you'll get feedback that challenges or disproves your assumptions. In this scenario, you'll form a new hypothesis based on the feedback, create a new experiment to test your new assumptions, and launch a new version. This method is directly in contrast with the instincts of many first-time founders, who often prefer to build their product in secret until it is exactly and perfectly what they think people want, without ever having validated this assumption. This can waste a lot of time and a lot of money.

There's even data to back up using the scientific method when starting a company. A study of entrepreneurs randomly assigned early-stage startup founders into a control group and test group.[3] Both groups received training on the Lean Startup method, but the test group was also trained to form hypotheses and rigorously test them on potential customers. Unsurprisingly, the entrepreneurs who operated like scientists were significantly more likely to realize their idea wasn't working early on and to pivot to a new idea than the control group. But here's the kicker: At the end of the study, the average revenue of the startups that behaved like scientists was over eight times higher than the average revenue in the control group!

One of the reasons thinking like a scientist is so effective is that it forces you to confront your assumptions and returns feedback in

---

3 Spina, C. (2020). "Founders, Apply the Scientific Method to Your Startup." *Harvard Business Review.* https://hbr.org/2020/11/founders-apply-the-scientific-method-to-your-startup

the form of data. If you're open to this method, you hopefully won't take it personally if your assumptions are wrong. When this happens, just dust yourself off and adjust by incorporating new data, designing a new experiment, and launching again. This will help you avoid the fate of the hardheaded founder who just "knows" their idea is right and refuses to adjust even when no one wants what they're selling.

Experimentation is key to survival. By being intentional about experimenting to get an answer, you ensure there is no such thing as failure—only learning. This thinking can apply to every aspect of your company: recruiting, product development, operations, team management, website design, and fundraising. The more you research, try, adapt, and repeat, the closer you will be to success.

DO YOUR HOMEWORK AND BUILD SOMETHING PEOPLE WANT

The simplest yet most insightful startup advice are these four words, attributed to Paul Graham, an entrepreneur and founder of the Y Combinator accelerator: *Build something people want.* Yet, the fact that it has to be said means there are a lot of founders starting companies who aren't building something people want. You may think you know what people want, but until you ask them, you can't be sure.

It's difficult to get an honest reaction to a new idea that people can't see, touch, experience, or interact with. Thus, it's important to build a minimum viable product (MVP) or a hacked-together prototype (ugly baby). The purpose of this first version is to create something people can react and provide feedback to. It will not be polished, beautiful, and perfect. To quote LinkedIn founder and venture capitalist Reid Hoffman, "If you are not embarrassed by the first version of your product, you've launched too late." What this means is that, until you are getting feedback from people on the basic concept, there is no reason to spend any time on it.

Your first iteration should be truly the minimum viable version or the ugliest baby. Most early physical product prototypes look like a bomb with ugly casings and wires hanging out. The goal is not to make something beautiful or perfect. The goal is to build something that gives you the opportunity to test your hypothesis about the value of what you're building.

This is often where many students and first-time founders get stuck. The best advice we can give you is keep moving! One of the biggest struggles we see at The Garage with engineering students and those with a predisposition for perfectionism is they fear their rough draft isn't good enough. They think they need to make one more improvement before releasing it. They get caught up in releasing the "perfect" product *eventually*, instead of a real product soon. Other students will get stuck in incessant planning: business plans, designs, go-to-market strategies, and any other plans that make the founder feel like they're doing work, without actually putting a product in the market.

If you and your team have a tendency to want to do one more survey, write a little more code, or solder a few more wires, stop. You need to validate as early as possible that you're building something that people want, and ironically, the best way to validate your big assumptions is with an imperfect version of your product. It sounds easier than it is. Perfect is the enemy of good. In building a company, time and feedback are two of your most important resources, and wasting time without getting feedback can be detrimental to your product development. So, take the time to get that all-important feedback. Trust us; it's worth every second.

BUILD A MINIMUM VIABLE PRODUCT TO TEST YOUR ASSUMPTIONS

Instead of trying to be perfect, channel that same energy and initiative into figuring out how you can hack together an MVP quickly. Can you repurpose an existing off-the-shelf product? Can you use inexpensive software to simulate what you want? Can you create a quick website based on a template? Can you create a nice 3D rendering or illustration? For example, if you're building an automated chat bot, can you simulate the experience with a human? Your goal is not to be deceptive. It is to build something that conveys your idea and is interactive.

Many students at The Garage build a website with mock-ups of their product or service well before they actually exist. Using their website, they create ads and run small-scale digital advertising campaigns for products that don't yet exist to test whether the product would have enough interest to efficiently acquire customers. Others have created Kickstarter or crowdfunding pages based on just their idea, even if they don't necessarily intend to actually go through with the fundraiser. Each of these exercises helps you gather feedback from strangers and potential customers to make sure you're on the right track.

GET LOTS OF FEEDBACK

Yes, it's time. You're ready to show your ugly baby to other people. You want to run a series of experiments and/or interviews to better understand how people respond to it. You'll want to have at least ten people use it. For example, if you are building a new alarm clock, you'll want to find ten volunteers to wake up using your product. You'll want to design a survey or interview to understand their experience, asking questions like *Did you like it? What didn't you like? How much better is this than your current alarm clock? How much would you pay to keep the prototype?*

Be sure to measure the level of value your beta users get from your product. Rate them on a scale of 0–3:

- 0: They are not interested.
- 1: They want it but aren't willing to pay for it (at least at your current price point).
- 2: They want it, and they'll pay for it.
- 3: They want it, they'll pay for it, and they'll tell their friends about it.

When you get consistent 3s, that's when you know you're onto something. You'll want to home in on that "killer feature," the moment when a user's or customer's eyes light up. This is the part of the experience they can't live without. While it's taken for granted now, the first time customers took an Uber and exited the vehicle without reaching for their wallet was mind-blowing and often prompted them to excitedly tell all of their friends about the experience.

TELL LOTS OF PEOPLE

Humans are complex. Sometimes potential users/customers will say they want one thing and then do something completely different. Good founders listen to their users/customers, but effective founders use emotional intelligence to go deeper into understanding their user's/customer's intentions, intonations, and desires. A skilled user/customer researcher will also observe voice tone and body language to better understand what the user/customer really wants and needs. If you aren't good at this, seek out a more intuitive team member to conduct your research.

As they say in the Valley, the best founders have "strong convictions, loosely held." You need to have conviction for what you're building, but you also need to be flexible in adapting the product to your customer and the market. One of the hardest parts of being an entrepreneur is incorporating feedback. Customers will ask for a feature and not use it. Two mentors with many years of experience and expertise will give contradictory advice. One of the hardest parts of being a founder is figuring out when you should take advice and when you should completely ignore it.

Some companies, like Slack, have a group of customers who agree to test new versions of the product and give honest feedback before the improvement is released more widely. Listening to your customers and incorporating their needs and wants into your product improvements is a necessity for long-term success and customer loyalty at every stage of development.

To succeed, you're going to need to tell a lot of people about your idea. The upsides of telling others about your idea are unlimited. For example, you may attract potential teammates who are interested in working on your idea. Mentors and advisors may have advice or connections to help you move your idea forward. And you may learn information about potential competitors or plans from incumbents.

Resist the urge to be guarded about your idea. First-time entrepreneurs and many student entrepreneurs often get very guarded about telling anyone their idea. It's counterintuitive, but, often, it's good to tell lots of people about your idea. Rarely will you find someone as passionate as you are that wants to steal your idea and will have the same grit, determination, and perseverance to turn your idea into a reality. Similarly, big companies in your industry move slowly and have other competing priorities, while, as a nimble startup with a singular focus, you can execute your idea much faster.

A common mistake of first-time founders is believing the idea is the valuable thing. They seem to believe that successful founders have one great idea that no one else has ever had and that, by being the first person to bring the idea into existence, they became successful. This belief makes them incredibly guarded with their idea and careful not to tell anyone they don't know and trust what they are working on. Some may ask anyone they speak with to sign a nondisclosure agreement (NDA) to make sure their idea isn't stolen. The hard reality for these individuals to accept is their idea, in itself, is worthless and that it is almost guaranteed to not be an original or unique one. In Silicon Valley, the heart of tech entrepreneurship in the US, founders pitch dozens of investors on their startup ideas, and yet, NDAs are a nonstarter for investors. Why? A founder who asks an investor to sign an NDA fundamentally misunderstands what their job is. Their job is not to *have* an idea; it's to *execute* that idea. Having worked in venture capital in Silicon Valley, Mike can tell you that no matter what your idea is, there are likely many other people working on something similar. Venture capitalists choose which companies to invest in based on which team they think has the highest potential to execute on their vision, not which team had the idea first.

Instead of being guarded with your idea, we suggest another approach: Tell everyone. Tell your family, friends, classmates, and colleagues. Post it on LinkedIn, Twitter, and Facebook. And reach out to experts or professionals who may have some thoughts or interest in what you're working on. If you're working on a technical product, share it on websites like Product Hunt. To succeed, you're going to need help from a lot of people, and the best way to find the right people is to cast a wide net and tell anyone who will listen. You'll be surprised where you will find your first customer or angel investor. If execution is everything, your job is to find the people who can help you execute.

SET GOALS THAT ARE MEASURABLE

Successful teams set goals. Why? Well, it's for a couple of reasons. First, goals give us something to strive for, which can motivate us to put in that extra time, to gather more feedback, or to send one more cold email. Having a stated goal also removes the trap of thinking you've done "enough" for today. If you haven't hit the goal, then keep going! Goals also serve another purpose. They align the team around a desired outcome.

Goals should be—

- Ambitious but attainable
- Specific and measurable
- Designed to include well-defined implementation plans
- Explicitly stated and shared by everyone on the team

One of the most difficult parts of setting goals is choosing the right ones. If your goal is too ambitious—let's say making $1 million in your first month—you and your team are quickly going to be deflated when you realize it's not attainable. Instead of this setback motivating them to put in a little extra effort, they'll all but give up, knowing that no amount of effort will get them to achieve this overly ambitious goal. On the other hand, if your goals aren't ambitious—let's say talking to one customer this week—they serve very little purpose and aren't motivating.

It's easy to set goals we know we can hit, and it's tempting to set optimistic goals that aren't achievable. The trick is to set goals that can be reached but that might be difficult to achieve.

Depending on your company, team, and stage, this could be earning your first $1,000 in revenue this month, talking to ten potential customers this week, or something else that will meaningfully impact your progress.

These examples are all specific and measurable, which leaves no doubt as to whether they've been reached or not. One mistake is choosing instead to use "softer" goals, which may include something like "improve the user onboarding flow" or "grow revenue." Lacking any quantifiable metrics, the smallest incremental improvement achieves the goal, which is not the point of goal setting. Instead, find ways to attach metrics to your goals. For instance, if your goal is to "improve the user experience," you could add "measured by improving the net promoter score (NPS) of new users from a score of 50 to a score of 65."

The next characteristic of productive goals is that they include implementation plans or defined strategies to reach them. If your goal is to "improve the user experience, measured by improving the NPS score of new users from a score of 50 to a score of 65," be specific about the strategies you're going to use to reach this goal. For example, "You'll improve your score by removing ads, decreasing load time, and adding recommendations." This forces you to be more thoughtful and intentional during the goal-setting phase. The more your practice this, the more you will get a feel for the levers you can (and can't) pull to make forward progress.

Finally, goals work best when everyone on your team is aligned with them. If goals are compartmentalized, individualized, or kept secret, you're robbing your team of both a collaborative and a motivational opportunity. One of the most special experiences of a startup is when everyone is pitching in to help, no matter their title or job. In this case, it's important to discuss your goals regularly with your team and update them on the company's progress. You could even post them in a public area or have a scoreboard displaying everyone's achievements.

It's important to understand that you're not going to reach every goal. If you do, that probably means that you're setting goals too low, and they could use a little more ambition!

IF YOU LEARN SOMETHING, YOU HAVEN'T FAILED

Initial products can fail for several reasons. Sometimes, it's because your product isn't better than the alternatives. Sometimes, the value the user or customer receives doesn't align with the prices you're charging. And sometimes, you're caught up in building something because you want to build something, not because anyone wants what you're building. It's possible that you're only building something that you want or a small group of your friends want. Or maybe you're solving a problem that only you have. Just because it's something you want people to want doesn't mean they'll actually want it.

Another pitfall for many startups is giving away their product for free or at a fraction of the price they would eventually need to charge to be profitable, fearing that people don't actually want the product they're selling. This can give you the false impression that people want what you're building, but in actuality, they're taking advantage of your subsidizing the product to an unrealistic level. It can also attract the wrong customer—for example, deal seekers interested in receiving a 90% discount and not customers that will eventually pay full price for your product or service. Don't wait to charge for the product or service you're offering. If customers want it, they'll pay for it. If they don't want to pay for it, perhaps you're not building the right thing.

Normalizing and embracing failure is essential as a founder, and it is a key part of the journey for entrepreneurs. You must build assumptions, test them, and iterate. You may open your business and have no one show up on the first day. You may launch your app in Apple's app store and get zero downloads. These are not failures. They are learning opportunities. Why didn't anyone show up or download your app? Your curiosity to figure it out must propel you forward. And the only way to learn is to fail forward.

ITERATE AND REPEAT

At the risk of *repeating* this point too many times, your job as an entrepreneur is not to come up with the perfect idea once and build that exact initial vision. Your job is to as quickly and inexpensively as possible test your assumptions, gather feedback, and iterate your product, solution, or customer base. We have never seen a student founder get it right the first time. The prototypes and different versions of your product are the first step in a long, iterative journey.

One final point we'd like to drive home is that this is a never-ending process. There will be no point in your company's journey where you stop iterating and working to improve your product. Netflix, founded in 1997, still runs millions of experiments every day to improve their product and customer experience. And now that you know how, just like Netflix, you'll be thinking like a scientist.

KEY TAKEAWAYS

- Entrepreneurship is an iterative process: hypothesize, test, learn, improve, repeat.
- Talk to potential customers before you build anything.
- Your first version should be very scrappy. Get feedback early and often.
- Tell/show lots of people; get their feedback.
- Set goals for yourself and your team that you can track.
- Learning isn't failing.

$$\textcircled{5}$$

KNOWING WHEN YOU'RE ONTO SOMETHING

At this point, you may be asking yourself, "But how do I know when I'm on the right track?" Great question! Through all of your experimentation, you'll likely see different results—more traffic on your website, people willing to pay (or pay more!) for your product or service, or more positive feedback from customers and users. The loose frameworks of problem–solution and product–market fit are milestones of customer traction that prove you have validated some of your assumptions and help you focus on what's next. To reach these milestones, you'll need to practice the advice from the end of last chapter: iterate and repeat.

To reach the first of these two early milestones, you will have validated both your assumptions around the problem with customer validation and research and your assumptions about your solution by building an MVP and getting it in front of customers.

The four questions you should be striving to answer early on are—

1. Who is your customer?

2. What problem are you solving for them?

3. Is your solution feasible?

4. Do your customers find your solution valuable?

How will you know if you've answered these questions satisfactorily? Easy! You'll have proof in the form of early customers willing to use or pay for your product or service, as well as positive feedback from them on your solution so far. At this point, your product won't be perfect (far from it!), but your early users will validate that you're on the right path and that they find some value in what you're building compared to the other solutions out there.

Akshat Thirani was a junior at The Garage when he had the idea to build a smart circuit breaker for homeowners and renters to understand their energy consumption at the appliance level. For example, if your coffee maker was drawing too much power while it was idle, a phenomenon called vampire power, you could unplug it when it was not in use. It's estimated that up to 20% of a monthly household electric bill is due to vampire power. After a chance encounter at a hackathon, Akshat received funding from the Thiel Fellowship to work on his project and built an initial prototype.

Although he was receiving a lot of external validation by winning pitch competitions and garnering investor interest, Akshat was privately worried that he couldn't actually find customers for his smart circuit breaker product who would find his solution valuable. Consumers didn't want it, because it was expensive to install and the energy savings were minimal. Landlords and property managers didn't think it would be a selling point to charge a higher rent price. Although his device could successfully solve the problem of monitoring a circuit breaker or appliance for any fluctuations in the amount of energy being drawn, there wasn't enough of a value proposition for a customer to buy his product. Akshat did not yet have problem–solution fit, and he knew it.

A visit home to his family in India led to a serendipitous moment, when his father, who managed factories, mentioned that he watches every penny spent on the factory floor. Akshat suddenly realized that he had been approaching the wrong customer and that manufactures would receive much greater value from his solution than individuals. Further research validated this assumption. Existing solutions were expensive and required a big installation. Akshat's device could be clipped onto the cord of a piece of manufacturing equipment and almost instantly display all kinds of information about the machinery for the factory manager.

After talking to potential manufacturing customers to get their feedback, Akshat evolved his solution for a new customer. He developed a factory operating system to monitor and

FOUNDED

manage manufacturing operations. Pretty quickly, Akshat achieved problem–solution fit and was able to raise a seed round of $3.5 million in funding from Silicon Valley venture capitalists.

Once you've reached problem–solution fit, a common mistake is to focus all of your resources on finding *more* customers in lieu of improving your product for *current* customers. This might be confusing. You may be thinking, "I've got people willing to pay for my product, which means there are probably others out there. Shouldn't I find them as soon as possible?" No! You've put in a lot of work to find your initial users, who are likely early adopters of new products and more forgiving of their shortcomings. But that doesn't mean they are completely delighted by your product or will be loyal customers indefinitely. Spending time and resources to bring in new customers to your early, scrappy MVP will likely leave those with higher standards disappointed. When you're focused on bringing in new customers to a product that isn't delighting current customers, this is known as a "leaky bucket." Someone may purchase or use your product once, but they aren't coming back. And it only gets more expensive to find new customers for an underdeveloped product.

Instead, once you've reached problem–solution fit, your next focus should be on listening to your existing customers, improving your product to better serve their needs, and adding features and functionality, which is known as "customer success," or making sure your earliest customers are satisfied with your improvements. The next milestone on your product journey is reaching product–market fit.

The concept of product–market fit was developed by Andy Rachleff, the founder and former CEO of Wealthfront and cofounder of storied venture capital firm Benchmark Capital. While there are many different descriptions of what constitutes product–market fit, three signals can be helpful to identify the milestone:

1. Your customers are delighted. (They're using/spending more and more.)

2. You have strong organic growth. (Customers are recommending your product to others.)

3. You need to dedicate more resources to keep up with inbound demand.

Put another way, you've reached product–market fit when growth is not your biggest problem; keeping up with demand is. Once you've achieved product–market fit, you can begin dedicating more resources to finding more customers (customer acquisition) and scaling your team to help grow your business.

After Amper raised their seed round of funding, Akshat moved the company from San Francisco to Chicago to be closer to more manufacturing customers and work closely with them to improve the original MVP to meet their needs. As his early customers became more delighted and satisfied and there was increasing interest from new potential customers, Akshat realized he had achieved product–market fit and was able to raise more venture capital to begin scaling the business. When students at The Garage ask us how they know when they've reached product–market fit, we tell them, "You'll know it when you see it." After months or years of toiling to get customers to use your product, you'll suddenly find yourself struggling to keep up with demand, and the difference will be palpable, just like in Akshat's story.

KEY TAKEAWAYS

- Problem–solution fit and product–market fit are early milestones to signal what to focus on next.
- Problem–solution fit is reached when you validate your assumptions around your customers and the value of your solution.
- After reaching problem–solution fit, focus on improving the product, not growth!
- Product–market fit is when keeping up with inbound demand is your biggest problem.
- Once you've reached product–market fit, it's time to scale!

BUILD YOUR PITCH

As an entrepreneur, one of your many jobs is to tell the story of your company and to customize this story to the audience you're speaking to at any moment—whether potential customers, investors, team members, or press. Storytelling is an imperative skill for entrepreneurs, because your job entails convincing talent to join your team, customers to try your product, and potentially, investors to invest in your company. Being able to succinctly tell a comprehensive and engaging story to all of these parties is a skill worth honing.

To be clear, this is not an exercise that you can complete in an afternoon by filling out a Mad Libs–style worksheet. Instead, this is an ongoing process of continuously thinking about, iterating, and A/B testing your startup story in conversations with other people to see what resonates the most. Your goal is to find the descriptions, anecdotes, and keywords that get people interested in your startup and excited about being a part of it.

When forming any story, one of the most beneficial traits to have is empathy, or the ability to put yourself in someone else's proverbial shoes and understand their perspective. Ask yourself, *What will the other person think about what I'm telling them and why? What are they motivated by? What are they afraid of? What are they looking for and why? How can my product or company help them?*

One broad framework to begin crafting your story is to—

1. Determine who you are trying to reach (your **audience**) and find out as much as you can about them.

2. Figure out what you want them to do: join your team, buy your product, invest in your company. That's the **goal**.

3. Think through the **challenges** that may get in the way of that goal: other job offers, less expensive competitive products, uncertainty of your capability.

4. Find or create a **character** to represent how someone might overcome those challenges.

5. Make sure there's a **resolution** to your story.

To make your story even more compelling, consider incorporating the following strategies when possible:

- **Tap into emotion**: Trigger an emotional response to provoke empathy in your audience.

- **Connect with your audience**: Use examples and situations that people can relate to.

- **Humanize yourself**: Offer a glimpse into who you are and what you value.

- **Raise the stakes**: Appeal to bigger themes and universal values.

- **Show; don't tell**: Demonstrate with an example instead of explaining.

PITCHING TO POTENTIAL EMPLOYEES

For potential employees, the most convincing story is often that your company has a worthwhile mission that they have the opportunity to join and that will allow them to contribute to something greater than themselves, in addition to building a product they love and believe in. Companies like Tesla and SpaceX can recruit top-tier talent because their missions are so big, clear, and aligned with their customers. Even if your company isn't solving the climate crisis or decreasing the cost of space travel, you can align your company and product with a larger mission: sustainability, saving people time, or unlocking human potential. This may take considerable time for you to develop. That's okay! While it's an extreme example, here's the pitch that Tesla uses on its careers website page:

> Tesla's mission is to accelerate the world's transition to sustainable energy. We hire the world's best and brightest people to help make this future a

> reality. . . . At Tesla, we're solving the world's most important problems with talented individuals who share our passion to change the world. Our culture is fast-paced, energetic, and innovative.

This is obviously clear, concise, and compelling to potential employees. It describes their higher mission, as well as their culture and workforce. But also notice that it doesn't even mention that they sell cars! Looking back at the strategies above, we'd say that this pitch to potential employees taps into emotion, connects us, raises the stakes, and humanizes the brand.

Of course, as a one-person startup, it's difficult to justify such a grandiose pitch to potential employees, but you should already be thinking about how to position the opportunity you're offering.

PITCHING TO POTENTIAL CUSTOMERS

Any and all communication or materials that you put out into the public says something about your brand, company, and values, which means it's extremely important to be intentional about your messaging. Generally speaking, customers want to know two things: First, they want to know that your product solves a problem for them and is better than other solutions in at least one aspect. Second, they want to know they will be proud to be associated with your brand, which brings us back to mission alignment. While much of this will be communicated via your sales and marketing efforts, you should also have a verbal pitch that you and any team member can make to any individual about why they should use your product. The most powerful customer pitches don't describe product features or capability. Instead, they demonstrate the power of your product through a story of how you've affected a customer's life. (Once again, show; don't tell!)

A great example of a customer pitch is from James Kubik, the cofounder and CEO of Somewear Labs, which makes satellite hot spots for adventurers:

> We had someone out on the Pacific Crest Trail, and they were getting toward the end of the trail, and they didn't have a way to get home. So they started using Somewear [James's product] to communicate logistics for their train ride home. They were literally booking tickets using the device. That person told us afterwards, "I wouldn't have been able to get out of there without Somewear."[4]

Notice that in four short sentences, James hits all five points of a powerful story listed above and demonstrates the value of his product through a story, not by dryly describing product features or capability. His story raises the stakes, taps into emotion, and shows instead of tells, ultimately helping any adventurer identify with the huge potential value of his product.

---

4 Arveson, A. (2019). "6 Questions for James Kubik, CEO of Somewear." *Outside Business Journal.* https://www.outsidebusinessjournal.com/brands/leaders/interview-james-kubik-somewear

PITCHING TO POTENTIAL INVESTORS

While pitching to investors and raising venture capital are beyond the scope of this book, there are plenty of resources and opinions on the subject online. It may be controversial, but we believe the vast majority of startups and small businesses founded by entrepreneurs don't need to—and, in fact, should not—chase investment from venture capitalists for a multitude of reasons. However, for the sake of this book, our goal is to help you get started, build a product, and begin gaining customer traction, all of which will make it much easier to find investors eventually.

If you do end up pitching to investors, your job is to craft a compelling and plausible story about why your company can succeed and scale to a big opportunity where others haven't. Most startup investors are interested in the potential for your company to scale to hundreds of millions of dollars per year in revenue, among other factors. Why do you have an unfair advantage? What's new in technology or consumer behavior that creates a new opportunity? What do you know that others don't (and why), and why are you uniquely skilled to execute on your vision?

When creating your pitch, don't think about it as checking off boxes or filling out a form (market, competition, business model, team). Instead, think of it more holistically. Ask yourself, *How can I convey my vision, unique insights, and the reasons I'll succeed over everyone else in a story they can remember and easily relay to other people?* This is a challenging feat, and you should temper your expectations. The vast majority of first-time founders will pitch to more than fifty investors before they receive a single "yes," and even that is on the low end.

Even if you don't succeed in every pitch to every audience (you won't), being intentional about crafting your story and putting in the reps will pay dividends in future projects and ideas for the rest of your life.

KEY TAKEAWAYS

- Storytelling is an important skill for entrepreneurs.
- Customize your story to your audience by understanding their perspective and motivations.
- Your story will continuously evolve.
- Use the five components of a powerful story to enhance your impact.

(7)

AVOIDING THE MOST COMMON FIRST-TIME FOUNDER MISTAKES

Having worked with thousands of first-time founders, we've seen the same misconceptions, pitfalls, and mistakes made over and over again and have compiled the three most common pitfalls of first-time founders. You will be talking to and working with many other people, and there will always be uncertainty. But you will need to overcome these pitfalls if you want to succeed. Some of the most common mistakes include—

1. Giving up too easily
2. Building something no one wants
3. Ignoring distribution

GIVING UP TOO EASILY

At The Garage, we often see students excitedly show up with an idea they want to get to work on, only to have them give up at the first sign of trouble. It might be they want to recruit an engineer to join their team but can't convince anyone. Or they heard from a few potential customers that they weren't interested in what they were building. Perhaps during their Warm-Up Lap, they found another product that was somewhat similar, became discouraged, and lost their motivation. All these things will happen at some point to every single project, but that does not mean they are doomed!

To avoid giving up on your idea too easily, we encourage you to set the right expectations going in, to be adaptable in your approach, and, most importantly, to have perseverance. Before you begin a new venture, it's important you have the right expectations about how much work it will take. For student founders, they're often juggling classes, extracurriculars, campus jobs, and a social life. For adults, the responsibilities and commitments in their lives are often even more demanding. Realize before you embark on this journey that it won't be easy. You're going to run into obstacle after obstacle, and you will need to be highly adaptable in your approach to clear the hurdles and move on to the next challenge.

Spencer Levitt and Austin Pager were two friends who loved competing with each other in video games such as Call of Duty and FIFA. Along with other friends in their fraternity, they would often engage in friendly bets or challenges in these games but were frustrated that there was no way for them to keep track of their stats or scores against each other besides recording them on paper. As they talked about it more, they believed there was an opportunity to build a product that automatically tracked their scores when they played against friends and recorded lifetime statistics, so they knew who had ultimate bragging rights. After doing some light research and hearing interest from their friends, Spencer and Austin were convinced there was a huge opportunity to create a social layer on top of their favorite games. There was only one problem: Neither of them was a software engineer.

For months, the duo tried to recruit student software engineers to join their team and build their product for them. When that didn't work, they decided to hire freelance engineers from the internet, which ended up costing a lot of time and money and did not deliver on their vision for the product. One freelancer disappeared after they had spent a month working with (and paying) him. At this point, they realized that nobody they could pay to build their product would ever care about it as much as they did.

Spencer says, "I started to think, 'Is it really so hard to build an app that all of these freelancers around the world have some crazy knowledge that I can't learn?' So I decided to start at the basics. I purchased a $9.99 Udemy course on making an app that was basically 40 hours of YouTube videos. I took notes throughout the course, and when it was over, I felt like I could actually code the app myself. Ten days later, we had the first working version of Qade."

It would have been easy for Spencer and Austin to give up after they had spent so much time and money trying to get Qade off the ground but still had nothing to show for it. Instead, they persevered and adapted, teaching themselves how to code, while demonstrating their commitment and conviction in their idea.

BUILDING SOMETHING NO ONE WANTS

We've already mentioned another common reason many startups fail, but it's worth repeating: They build something that nobody wants. While this isn't revelatory in itself, there are two fundamental reasons first-time founders make this mistake: Either they are too stubborn about their initial idea or they are too guarded about what they're working on and fail to get feedback in the earliest stages.

Being too stubborn

Founders who believe the idea is the most valuable thing (rather than execution, aka thinking like a scientist) often struggle to be adaptable in their approach and pivot when all signs are saying that their original idea is not going to work. Typically, these hard headed founders are so convinced that their original vision is correct that they ignore all the feedback and data that say otherwise. This failure to accept reality can cost precious time, money, and team morale.

It's important to understand from the get-go that things aren't going to work out exactly how you expect them to. Your initial idea is not going to be exactly the one that people want. An imperative skill for any entrepreneur is adaptability—figuring out a new angle or product or distribution channel when the current one isn't successful. If you embrace thinking like a scientist, you shouldn't fall victim to being too stubborn.

When Spencer and Austin finally released Qade, they ran into their next hurdle:

> The app worked. But the big problem with Qade after seven or eight iterations was that people were excited by the idea but didn't continue to use the product over time. That is what propelled us to start asking questions like "What did we learn from this?" and "Where do we go from here?"
>
> So we asked users what got them excited about it initially, why they stopped using it, and all those questions. What we ended up discovering was that they liked seeing whether their friends won or lost video games and commenting on it but didn't care about betting, which was a major component of the original app.
>
> So we took that discovery and made a new app called Buff'd while still running Qade. Buff'd was built in a week, and we quickly got 100 people on the app who liked the product and continued to use it.

Instead of doubling down on Qade or spending more time and money trying to get users onto the app, Spencer and Austin realized their initial idea might not be as compelling as they thought it was. By talking to their users and asking them questions, they avoided building something no one wanted and were able to build a product that people actually did want.

Being too guarded about your idea

Another reason founders end up building something that nobody wants is they fail to gather input and feedback from potential customers from the earliest stages, often out of a fear of embarrassment or negative feedback. These founders will spend months building their product in private, afraid to show or tell anyone what they're working on until it is "perfect." When they finally launch or release their product, they're shocked to find that the people they thought would want it actually aren't interested. For many, this is a heartbreaking letdown, and they may decide to shutter the project.

To avoid this mistake, we recommend talking to people in your targeted customer segment from the very beginning to hear directly from them what they are interested in. Share each new iteration and version of your product with anyone who will take a look. Ask for honest feedback, what's missing, and what they do or do not like, just like Spencer and Austin did with Qade. While you shouldn't put too much weight on any individual opinion, talking to a lot of people you consider potential customers should give you directional input on what to build.

In addition to making sure you're building something people want, there's another reason you shouldn't be shy or guarded about your project. For your startup to be successful, you're going to need a lot of help from a lot of people. You're going to need to build a talented team, you're going to need customer input and feedback, you're going to need relationships with suppliers or buyers or partners, and you may end up needing investors to grow your company.

Your chances of finding the best people to help you along your journey are much, much higher if you tell anyone and everyone what you're building and what you need help with. Tell your friends, family, and classmates. Post about it on your social media channels. Start a blog! The more people who know what you're building and what you need help with, the better your odds of getting the best help from the best people.

One of the things you'll discover with this strategy is how serendipitous being an entrepreneur can be! Your friend from middle school that you haven't spoken to in years may see your tweet about hiring a designer and connect you to a very talented designer they know. A stranger on the internet may read your blog post and reach out to discuss investing in your company. Or maybe your mom's boss has been looking for the software you're building and comes on board as a beta customer. All of these things are only possible if you tell people what you're building. But if you don't tell anyone, no one can help you. So, don't be shy!

IGNORING DISTRIBUTION

One of the most overlooked components of a new product or service by first-time founders is distribution, or your go-to-market plan. In other words, how do you get your product in front of your potential customers? "If you build it, they will come" is simply not true when it comes to new products or services. It's not uncommon for first-time founders to spend months building out a website and launching it, only to realize there's no reason anyone would know about it or be able to find it. It happens with physical products, software, service companies, nonprofits, and every other type of creation. It can be incredibly discouraging to put all the time and effort into creating something, only to have no one show up once you launch it.

At the earliest stages, it's important to find ways to get your product in front of potential customers organically (without paying for ads), even if it costs a lot of time or effort on your part. Not only can advertising be expensive, but if users don't already love your product, it can be a complete waste of money if the users you pay for stop using or buying your product. You should begin exploring how to do this even before your product is ready by thinking about two questions: (1) Who are my target customers/users, and (2) where do they spend their time? This could be physical places (e.g., college campuses) or virtual places (i.e., where they spend their time online).

Finding a unique distribution plan will be critical to your success. Facebook's initial distribution strategy through college campuses was novel at the time. Since then, it's been replicated many times, including by Bumble, which launched through college fraternities and sororities. RXBAR found an enthusiastic early adopter audience through CrossFit gyms.

Like these successful companies, you'll want to dedicate time to brainstorming which channels and communities would be the best fit for your product. Be creative and look in niche communities that are the right fit for your audience or emerging platforms that are yet to be discovered by the mainstream. Consider working with social media influencers or even micro influencers on newer social media platforms or long-tail content creators experimenting with new forms of content.

At The Garage, many of our student teams find their first customers in online communities organized around interests relevant to their product. This could be a subreddit, Facebook group, or even the Nextdoor app to find local users. Others post flyers around campus or at local shops, speak in front of relevant student organizations, or recruit their friends on other college campuses to be ambassadors for the product on their campuses.

When Spencer and Austin first built Qade, their first users were their friends and other fraternity members on campus. But the duo was committed to finding as many users as possible without paying for them, so they kept at it.

We literally went through every single phone number in our contacts and texted them on the off chance they played games or knew someone who played video games. It was definitely awkward reaching out to some people you haven't spoken to since middle school, but we definitely got a lot of users doing that.

When they pivoted to Buff'd, Spencer and Austin thought more intentionally about who their ideal users were and where they spent their time.

> For Buff'd, we're building a product that people who spend a lot of time gaming would like. Who are those people? Easy, Twitch streamers. How do we get in touch with Twitch streamers? Let's just go on their streams and talk to them. We would go on Twitch, sort streams by popularity from low to high. We'd go into the streams with zero viewers, and the streamers would get really excited when someone comes to talk to them. So we'd chat with them for a few minutes, comment on their game play, and then say, "I'm working on this project I think you might enjoy, would you mind checking it out?" Usually they would end up download-ing it and then inviting their friends on as well. And that's how our community started being built.

We'll discuss distribution in more detail later in the book, but an important point highlighted by Spencer and Austin is that to get their first customers, they engaged in activities that don't scale. Buff'd probably won't get 1 million customers from the two founders texting their contacts and individually talking to Twitch streamers with no viewers, but it did succeed in getting their first 1,000 users, and all it cost them was time and creativity.

You'll also want to experiment with other alternative tactics. Uber's growth was augmented by its referral program, for example. Gmail and Slack utilized exclusive invite-only scarcity models. Other ideas include competitions, posting in forums, or piggybacking off an existing community. For example, Dropbox created a viral video full of memes for the Digg community, and Airbnb sent targeted emails to people posting short-term rentals on Craigslist.

Even before your product is ready, it's important to design, test, and build a strategic go-to-market plan that gets your product in front of customers at scale. Create a plan that utilizes several strategies, including niche communities, partnerships, sales, media exposure, content, referral programs, advertising, or some other distribution channel. Finding the right distribution channels will require a lot of trial and error. Use your thinking-like-a-scientist mindset to find the right channels for your business. It will be crucial to your eventual success!

KEY TAKEAWAYS

- Don't give up too easily! Have perseverance and adapt.
- Make sure you're building something people want.
- Don't be shy! Tell everyone what you're working on.
- Be considerate and intentional about how you'll get in front of customers.

PERSONALITY TRAITS OF SUCCESSFUL ENTREPRENEURS

After six years of working with student founders at The Garage, we observed many similarities of successful student founders. We decided to conduct our own research to see if there were personality traits that made someone more likely to succeed as an entrepreneur. Interestingly, there is very little academic research on personality traits of entrepreneurs and even less so on successful entrepreneurs.

We teamed up with Jennifer L. Tackett, PhD, a psychology professor at Northwestern with expertise in the field of personality assessment, to conduct a study on successful entrepreneurs. To define *success*, we set the bar pretty high, because we thought there might be a difference between people who call themselves successful entrepreneurs (wantrepreneurs) and those who have achieved the outcomes to prove success. The participants in our study have founded or cofounded a company and scaled it from a startup to multimillions of dollars in revenue. Most have experienced either a significant exit or taken the company public. Our preliminary finding analyzed twenty-six successful entrepreneurs.

We're going to discuss the personality traits that are correlated with these successful entrepreneurs in our study, but we want to make one thing clear: If you don't fit this profile, it doesn't mean you can't be a successful entrepreneur. X-Factor, our groundbreaking leadership development cohort program developed by The Garage and Dr. Tackett, does not advise students who don't share this profile that they won't succeed. Instead, we use it as an opportunity to identify the likely strengths, weaknesses, and blind spots of our student entrepreneurs while helping them identify traits and strengths they will want to seek out in cofounders and teammates to bolster their likelihood of success.

In the words of Katie Hoffman, a student in our X-Factor program, "X-Factor taught me more than I could have ever expected. It gave me the self-awareness and confidence to really put myself out there and publish my own podcast. I finally learned what my strengths and weaknesses are in a meaningful way."

The Hogan Leadership Forecast Series (LFS) is hands down the most scientifically sound personality assessment for management potential, which we adapted to study successful entrepreneurs and foster self-awareness in our student entrepreneurs. The LFS assessment is used by more than 75% of Fortune 500 companies and has been extensively used for leadership selection and development at the highest levels of these businesses. However, what is surprising is that very little is known about how the LFS might generalize to other types of business contexts, such as entrepreneurship. Therefore, we set out to address this important question: When the LFS is given to successful entrepreneurial leaders, are we able to identify key aspects of personality that might characterize successful entrepreneurs more broadly?

HIGH AMBITION AND SOCIABILITY, LOW PRUDENCE

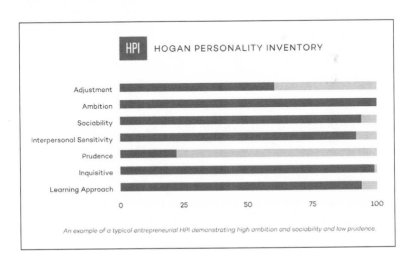

An example of a typical entrepreneurial HPI demonstrating high ambition and sociability and low prudence.

Our proprietary research revealed that, on average, the successful entrepreneur in our study is someone who is very ambitious and sociable, which perhaps is not too surprising, but it is one of the first academic studies verifying these correlations. Ambitious individuals tend to have a high level of self-confidence, tend to identify as leaders, and are competitive and highly energetic. Sociable individuals tend to be high in their individual needs for social interaction and tend to enjoy social situations, such as group meetings and parties. It makes sense that our successful entrepreneurs are high in both. These characteristics are likely very adaptive in the fast-paced, competitive startup world, where success is dependent on interpersonal interaction like speaking to and building a customer base and pitching to employees and investors.

Even more dramatic than the high scores for ambition and sociability is what appears to be the quintessential trait. By far, the overwhelming majority of our successful entrepreneurs scored very low on the personality trait labeled "prudence." High prudence reflects the degree to which an individual is conscientious, dependable, structured, and prone to following rules. Low prudence indicates a risk taker who thinks outside the box and is able to pivot quickly and thrive in ambiguity. Instead of accepting things for what they are, the successful entrepreneur is more likely to ask "but why?" Questioning the reasons behind why the world is the way it is or why a product doesn't exist or why we do things the way we do can unlock enormous potential for change.

These early findings suggest that successful entrepreneurs are largely similar and have high ambition and sociability and low prudence. Now, you may be reading this and thinking that you're not that sociable or that you typically follow the rules and may have high prudence. (We're going to assume that you're pretty ambitious since you picked up this book.) Are you doomed to fail and never become a successful entrepreneur? Not in the least! First, these traits are not universal, and there are exceptions—even in our own data!

But more importantly, no startup reaches success with the work of just one person. If you're going to go the distance, you'll need a team around you and, most likely, some early cofounders to get your startup off the ground. The best cofounding teams that we see at The Garage have a diversity of talent, knowledge, and—you guessed it—personalities.

KEY TAKEAWAYS

- In our research, successful founders have high ambition and sociability and low prudence.
- The best cofounding teams have a diversity of talent, knowledge, and personalities.

(9)

FINDING THE RIGHT COFOUNDERS

Entrepreneurship can be a lonely, difficult journey, but finding a cofounder or two can make that journey more bearable and fun. It's imperative that you're intentional about who you bring on board to be your cofounder. If your commitment, vision, and priorities aren't aligned, your venture is already in jeopardy.

Cofounders are like the captains of the ship. They are leaders responsible for the voyage, and if the ship goes down, they should be the last ones off the boat. Founders are often the original visionaries and core team that took the concept from idea to business. Most startups have two (Larry and Sergey from Google) or three cofounders (Brian, Nathan, and Joe from Airbnb). Student founders tend to bring on too many cofounders too quickly. We recommend no more than three cofounders, unless you have a very good reason.

Finding a cofounder or cofounding team can be a great way to round out the skill sets and personality strengths of your team. At The Garage, we prefer all teams that participate in our incubation program or summer preaccelerator program to have at least two team members. We believe this is important, because it's a great first test to see if you can convince at least one other person that your idea is worth working on. Sometimes, the second person is a cofounder; other times, it's an early team member. Either way, it's an early signal that you can at least explain your idea to someone else and get them invested in working on it. We find that in addition to more brain power and complementary skills, teams of two can motivate each other and balance the emotional impact of setbacks. When one team member is feeling demoralized or down, the other team member often jumps into motivation mode—something solo founders miss out on.

Picking a cofounder is as serious as picking a spouse or partner. You shouldn't make a big commitment to someone without knowing that you work well together, have the same ethics, and have a similar vision for your project. When you enter a legally binding agreement, which you will do with your cofounder, you're contractually obligated to that person for a very long time.

At the same time, one of the most common mistakes we see student founders make at The Garage is choosing their close friends as their cofounders or teammates. More than a few friendships have fallen victim to the cofounder commitment problem at The Garage. While at the earliest stages of a startup this may sound like a fun idea, it is often revealed pretty quickly that one person is more invested in the startup than the other, who either hasn't prioritized the project as high as the original founder or really just wants to be able to tell people that they're a "cofounder." When the workload is lopsided, the original founder faces a conundrum: Do they hold their friend accountable for not putting in the work? Do they kick them off the team? Or do they let it slide and let this lack of dedication become an early part of the company culture?

The typical startup takes eight to ten or more years from idea to exit. Many take even longer. The majority will flame out long before an exit. Either way, when you choose a cofounder, you're committing to a very big adventure together full of very high highs and very low lows. So, choose wisely.

Before you invite someone to join you on the entrepreneurial journey, it's imperative that you're on the same page about expectations, prioritization, and commitment. At The Garage, we encourage students to talk with radical candor about their commitment to working on a project. We recommend taking time to get to know your potential cofounders and to have transparent, honest conversations. You can find extensive questionnaires and resources online on this topic, but some key topics to be on the same page about are—

- How much time can you dedicate to this project on top of classwork?

- Do you have a shared set of values and goals?

- Do you trust and respect each other?

- What is your style for handling disagreements and disputes?

- Are you passionate about the problem you are solving?

- How much time and money are you willing to dedicate to the project?

- How does the priority of this project compare to other priorities in your life?

- How will you split responsibilities?

- Who will have decision-making power on spending money and selling the company?

- What if someone wants to take another job?

- Would you drop out of school if the idea was taking off?

- What are your expectations for the company?

- Is this a lifestyle business, a small business, a side hustle, or a venture-backable company?

- Why do each of you want to commit to this (e.g., to learn, to make money, for the title, to solve the problem)?

You want to seek out a cofounder with a shared vision and values who also has complementary skills. One example of this is the hacker, hipster, and hustler triad. The hacker is the technical person, usually an engineer. The hipster is the designer. The hustler is the business-minded salesperson. One example is Brian, Joe, and Nathan of Airbnb. This trio of skills is especially important for a technology company; it may be less important for, say, a climate change nonprofit. The takeaway is that a diversity of skill sets is important for any founding team. Ask yourself which skills are critical for what you're working on, and see how you stack up. If all the skills aren't covered in the cofounding team, make sure it's accounted for in your early teammates.

At The Garage, we host a quarterly event called Startup Matchmaking, where student founders pitch their ideas to a room full of students looking to join a startup. Each team describes what they're building (their product, vision, and values) and what type of help they're looking for (engineers, designers, or marketers).

One of the reasons this event is so successful at matching students to startups is the diversity of talent and skills in the room: journalism students sitting next to engineers and business school students, among every other concentration. By exposing both the vision of the startup and the complementary skills they're looking to bring on board, the startups that pitch are flooded with interest from students who believe in their vision and have the skills they're looking for. Notably, these new team members usually aren't someone that they'd ever run into or meet at school if it weren't for Startup Matchmaking.

As was demonstrated in our research on successful entrepreneurs, there's also a benefit to cofounders that have different personality traits or complementary strengths and weaknesses. In many cofounding relationships, there is an anchor and a balloon.

Usually, one cofounder is the visionary. This is the person with the crazy, large vision that is challenging the norm. This is the one who says things like, "Let's build rockets and go to Mars! Let's cure cancer! Let's solve climate change!" This person is usually good at dreaming up the impossible and rallying the team to get there. In our research, these are the quintessential low-prudence founders. We call this person the balloon.

But every balloon needs an anchor to keep it grounded to Earth. This is the cofounder that sees the vision, breaks it down into smaller goals, and makes a plan to get there. This person is usually good at dotting the i's and crossing the t's. In our research, these founders usually have higher prudence. Sometimes, this dynamic is between cofounders. Other times, it's between a founder and a senior executive. Examples include Elon Musk (balloon) and Gwynne Shotwell (anchor) at SpaceX or Mark Zuckerberg (balloon) and Sheryl Sandberg (anchor) at Facebook.

Some founders choose to be solo founders or find themselves as a solo founder if their cofounders leave the venture. Being a solo founder is difficult. Those who do choose this route will still need to bring on an inner circle of advisors, executives, and senior employees with a diversity of skills.

It will take a small village of people for your idea to have any chance of success. Beyond your cofounders, you'll need employees, mentors, advisors, investors, and an army of friends and family to support you. It's important that you surround yourself not just with good people but also with the right people. The right people will be interested in your idea for the right reasons: They will believe in you and what you're building. This is the most important factor for your cofounders. But not everyone is the right fit. Don't pick people based purely on proximity or talent. Be very clear on the motivations, intentions, and desired outcome for your cofounders and early team members.

FOUNDERS' AGREEMENTS

So you think you've found the right one or two cofounders and are ready to take it to the next level. Now what? Remember all of that emphasis on radical candor and transparent, honest conversations? Well, we're about to turn up the heat!

A founders' agreement (or operating agreement) is a legally binding contract that outlines the roles, rights, and responsibilities of each owner in the business. These agreements form the foundation of how your cofounder relationships will work in the future, how your company is structured, and what each cofounder contributes to the business. It will also outline negative scenarios that might occur with actions to help avoid them or mechanisms to govern such situations. It does not matter what kind of business entity you are forming (e.g., C-Corp, S-Corp, LLC, or limited partnership). These concepts apply to all business types.

The founders' agreement is for the cofounders and is a reference for when—and particularly (but not exclusively) if—a conflict arises. Some elements of this document may spill over into other business paperwork like the articles of organization that we'll discuss later. However, this document is not required by law to form a business.

We should mention that founders' agreements can be oral, but such an oral agreement is often an invitation for future dispute, as founders disagree about the nature of the original oral agreement, and the likelihood for dispute increases exponentially if the company later becomes successful. Therefore, to avoid a negative outcome, we strongly encourage you to put together a written founders' (or operating) agreement as early as possible to avoid potential disputes later on, especially when the company has little or no value.

There are lots of founders' agreement templates available online. You can also work with an attorney, or you can draft a simple one on your own. The Garage works with a number of attorneys who specialize in preparing these types of documents. Scott Schonfeld[5] of Fox Swibel Levin & Carroll assisted in edits of this chapter and has worked with a number of startups that started in The Garage, including Brewbike. As a general rule, having something in writing is better than having nothing. We recommend looking at templates available online and picking the one that you feel is best for your team. If you can afford to do so, we strongly encourage having an attorney prepare or review it before having all cofounders sign it.

It's best to draft your founders' agreement early, when things are going well and everyone is excited to work together. We recommend the lock-in approach, where all cofounders meet in person and don't leave the room until the agreement is done. This may require several sessions, so wear your comfy pants, and bring lots of snacks!

---

5   Scott can be reached at SSchonfeld@foxswibel.com or
    https://foxswibel.com/who-we-are/scott-a-schonfeld

Founders' agreements typically address the following topics:

- Company goals
- Roles and responsibilities of each cofounder
- Ownership structure and equity breakdown
- Vesting schedules for equity grants
- Protection of intellectual property
- Management of the company (e.g., manager vs. member managed)
- Restrictive covenants (such as noncompetition or nonsolicitation clauses)
- Dispute resolution and/or exit mechanisms (e.g., put/call, shotgun buy/sell, and litigation)

What's most important in this process is having the hard conversation and getting everyone to come to an agreement. It forces you to think through worst-case scenarios and decide what you would do before they happen or what occurs when such events do transpire. Writing this down in a founders' agreement and having all cofounders sign it is the way to legally memorialize this conversation, so there's no ambiguity on what everyone has agreed to.

EQUITY

One topic you will need to address in your founders' agreement is how you will divide up the ownership of the business. Splitting equity is one of the most complex and controversial startup topics.

There are a wide range of thoughts and opinions on this subject. Some experts think all cofounders should split the equity evenly, regardless of dollars contributed or effort exerted. Others use complex calculators that take into account elements like the amount of money contributed or time spent on the startup and job title to crunch the percentages.

Different teams have different ways of splitting the equity. Some do it at the very beginning, and others go through a trial period first. Some teams use a negotiation process, and others do it quickly and agree with a handshake. Each cofounding team and business is unique, so you'll need to determine what's right for your team.

Regardless of how you choose to do it, we encourage you to be thoughtful. This may be one of the first stressors of your cofounding team, and how you handle it can be indicative of future success. At the end of the day, this is about relationships and trust. Your negotiation should reflect this. Research also suggests that startups that have lengthier and more robust dialogue around equity splits are more successful over time.

This decision has the potential of triggering a lot of hard and difficult emotions, especially when you're relying on everyone to discuss their potential, what they feel they are worth, and matching that to an actual equity share. If you use the lock-in method, we recommend using that forum as the culmination of a much longer dialogue about equity. For that reason, we recommend working together first and taking your time with the equity-splitting process.

Before we dive in, you should note: Student founders get really hung up on equity. We've seen friendships ruined and ideas abandoned simply because the cofounders couldn't agree on how to split equity. As we've stated earlier, the value of an idea is $0. Usually, even after you've done some preliminary mock-ups or customer discovery, it's still worth $0! It will all come down to execution to create any monetary value and years of hard work to turn that equity into cash. Therefore, when the business is first getting started, try to remember that the equity you're tempted to fight over isn't worth anything . . . yet. So, whether you have 5% or 95% of the equity in a business, in the beginning, it's worth $0. Since most startups fail, we'd hate for you to lose a friendship over $0 of equity.

However, for the very lucky few founders who are successful, that equity can be worth a life-changing amount of money. The difference between owning 5% and 95% of a billion-dollar company is astronomical. Therefore, equity is not a topic to be taken lightly. So, just in case this is you, here are some ideas on how to address this topic.

Splitting equity

Equity is the most valuable resource you have as a founder. It is a literal piece of your business! You should only give equity to people who are critical to the business, like cofounders, key hires, and, down the road, a small pool for employees and advisors. The artist who painted a mural at Facebook's original headquarters was paid in equity. Those stock options were valued at $200 million at Facebook's IPO!

One caveat: Do not use it as a form of compensation unless you have to! In this example, either skip the office mural or find a way to pay in cash. Once you give away equity, it's hard or impossible to get it back. We recommend that you split up 90% of your equity up front between cofounders. The other 10% can be reserved for future hires and other circumstances. As Lucas Phillips, who cofounded Brewbike as a college student at The Garage, put it, "The less equity you distribute in the beginning, the more optionality you will have in the future, whether it be a sale of the business, fundraising, raising debt, or bringing on an experienced partner."

But what about teammates who want equity? We hate to say it, but the vast majority of your founding team will leave you. Hopefully, teammates will be happy to contribute for a good professional experience and a résumé bullet point. If that's the case, get it in writing. If you can pay them, you can hire teammates as interns, employees, or contractors. But do some research first on local employment laws for the nuances of each type of categorization. If the contribution was really substantial, perhaps you could consider giving them a token of equity, but we'd recommend no more than 1% max. In an established Silicon Valley startup, 1% of equity is considered big and is usually reserved for very strategic hires.

Student founders often get into trouble in a few ways, but the root of all of these problems is when someone is allocated a big chunk of equity and then walks away. This happens all of the time for student founders. Students, by definition, are in school, and a lot can change in a few years, even for the most dedicated student founders. Therefore, when dividing equity, we encourage you to prioritize the longevity of the business. What's the right equity split for the long-run success of the company and not your pocketbook? How do you prevent the business from suffering if a cofounder who has a large piece of equity leaves the company?

Let's consider an example of four cofounders who split the equity equally at the beginning, so they had 25% each. If one of the cofounders decides to leave after a few months, this will have terrible consequences. The most problematic consequence is that the departing cofounder owns 25% of the company and won't be contributing! This scenario will make it impossible for this company to raise money from investors, because investors don't like absentee founders. Usually, the cofounder who is leaving feels entitled to the equity and won't give it back. This is crippling to the business, regardless of the success of the product or service, and everyone's equity will end up being worthless.

We don't have a firm recommendation on how you should split the equity. We've seen teams be successful with an even split between cofounders, as well as with an uneven split. What's important is that the split feels fair to all members of your team. Regardless of what you choose, we do recommend that one of the cofounders have more equity than the other, even if it's just 1%. The reason is that an even split means that all of the cofounders will need consensus to make any decisions about the company. An uneven split ensures a tie breaker and a decision-maker. Usually, the cofounder serving as the CEO should serve this role, but it may vary, depending on the team.

Besides picking the right cofounders, building a lot of trust, and dividing the equity fairly, we recommend that any grants of equity to non-full-time founders follow a vesting schedule. A vesting schedule means that equity owners earn their equity over time by actively contributing to the startup or by achieving predetermined milestones (e.g., sales/revenue/profit targets).

Some vesting schedules have a cliff. A cliff means you have to work for the company for a specific period of time before you earn any equity. A traditional schedule is four years with a one-year cliff, meaning, after the one-year point, 25% of your stock has vested and every month thereafter, an additional 1/48th of your total stock vests as hard equity. You only earn all of your stock at the end of four years. Depending on your situation, you may want to set a different cliff or schedule. For example, you might want to align the cliff with graduation, so if anyone leaves the startup for a job, you haven't given away any equity.

In summary, take your time when deciding how to split equity between cofounders. Consider not splitting equity equally so consensus between all cofounders is not required. Generally, the cofounder serving as CEO should have the most equity, even if it's just a 1% difference in a two-person cofounding team. Use a vesting schedule with a cliff to make all cofounders earn equity over time. Anticipate that one or more cofounders will leave, and ensure that a departure doesn't mean sacrificing the long-term success of the business or its ability to fundraise down the road. Finally, equity is your most valuable resource, so be careful with how and to whom you allocate it.

KEY TAKEAWAYS

- Take your time to find the right cofounders, and have transparent, honest conversations to ensure you have a shared vision and values.

- A founders' agreement is a legally binding contract that outlines the roles, rights, and responsibilities of each cofounder in the company.

- Be thoughtful about how you divide equity; consider a vesting schedule with a cliff.

BUILDING AN ENTREPRENEURIAL MINDSET AT ANY AGE

We believe working on an entrepreneurial project in college or graduate school is valuable, but younger students can get a head start in high school or even middle school. Remember, you get stronger with more reps, so starting early is an advantage. No one expects a middle school or high school student to build a billion-dollar company, although kudos to you if you do! Instead, the advice is the same. Leverage your skills, interests, and talents. A lawn care company, website development business, dog walking service, and jewelry company are all great places to start.

Daniel Green and Marianne Zapata started their business, Beyond Natural and Co., the summer before their senior year of high school. Beyond Natural and Co. is a meal prep business that offers healthy, nutritious meals for health-conscious clients.

Marianne works at a gym and has a passion for fitness, nutrition, and bodybuilding. She invited her boyfriend, Daniel, to start working out and training with her. They enjoyed cooking together and making healthy and nutritious meals that complemented their fitness lifestyle. They wondered if they could turn their passion for healthy cooking into a business by making it easier for other people to live a healthier lifestyle too.

To test the idea, they created an Instagram account and a promo video. They added photos of fifteen of their favorite healthy meals. They quickly started to get a lot of attention from their peers, classmates, and neighbors. "We were expecting three or four clients when we launched," said Daniel. They were happily surprised to get eight clients at launch. All of them were strangers, except Daniel's mom.

Daniel and Marianne outgrew their parents' kitchens after the pilot and have since been preparing meals in a commercial kitchen. Today, they prepare hundreds of meals a week for their clients. One of their favorite meals is a healthy spin on *bandeja paisa*, a nod to Marianne's Colombian roots, a dish with ground steak, plantain, veggies, and beans.

Daniel and Marianne are a great team. They've figured out each of their respective strengths and weaknesses. Marianne has a talent for recipe development and customer relations. Daniel has a talent for back-end operations like managing spreadsheets and their website. They develop the menu together and enjoy bouncing ideas off each other.

Their advice to other students and young founders is to keep pushing through the ups and downs.

"As long as you give it your all, you can be successful. The most important thing is that you are passionate and love what you do," said Marianne. "Don't be afraid to go after it," added Daniel.

In another example, Sam Kim Jr. started his first business in seventh grade, when he realized his peers prioritized not being themselves in order to fit in and be popular. Soon enough, his solution came to fruition, and Be Fly, a business that made apparel products that made it "cool to be you," was born. All the designs and apparel were made by Sam himself and, thanks to his main value proposition, 20% of Be Fly's revenue went right back into helping struggling members of his community. With the help of his parents, thirteen-year-old Sam saw his idea go from an art project to cash in his—and his community's—pocket.

As a college student at Northwestern, Sam incubated three entrepreneurial projects at The Garage, including Backlight, a service that combined seasoned copy editors with artificial intelligence to optimize résumés; Care Package, a college student snack and supplies delivery company; and Retriever, a peer-to-peer service for finding lost items on campus. While none of these businesses made it out of The Garage, Sam admittedly learned more than he would have through any class about business, engineering, and operations just by going out and doing it.

Outside of The Garage, Sam realized that problem-solving was not only a passion but also a key skill for success in entrepreneurship, so naturally, he chose to study math and physics. Once it was time to consider a career, the high-paying technologist jobs at big tech companies interested him, but they seemed too large and slow-moving to justify starting his career there. Nonetheless, after some soul-searching and careful considerations, he found a unique career path that was better aligned with his interests, talents, and lifestyle. Little did he know that his lifelong hobby—fishing—would manifest into his first job out of college.

After graduation, Sam joined Catch Co., a subscription-based outdoor e-commerce company, as a data strategist. He was able to combine his classwork in math and physics, his interest and experience in startups, and his passion for fishing into the perfect first professional role. Catch Co. provided Sam with the responsibility, learning opportunities, and fast pace while he could still enjoy long weekend fishing trips.

It's never too early to embrace an entrepreneurial project, but younger founders will need help from a parent or guardian. Minors under eighteen years old need help with tasks like setting up a legal business entity and opening a business bank account. Luckily for Sam, his parents introduced him to entrepreneurship early on, which gave him the breadth of experience necessary to learn and work on many different things.

As Daniel, Marianne, and Sam have demonstrated, taking opportunities to learn in stride often leads to entrepreneurial experiences, which compound and can take your life and career in unexpected directions. The sooner you start to embrace this mindset, the better.

YOU'RE NEVER TOO OLD TO GET STARTED

Although the glamorization of entrepreneurs is typically focused on young wunderkinds like Whitney Wolfe Herd, cofounder of Bumble and the world's youngest self-made billionaire, and Mark Zuckerberg, cofounder of Facebook, the reality is the vast majority of entrepreneurs do not get their start so young. In fact, according to one Harvard Business Review study, people with decades of professional experience are much more likely to start a company and be successful with their venture.[6]

So, just because you did not start your first company as a teenager does not mean you won't become a successful entrepreneur. Professional experience and knowledge, especially in the industry that you choose to launch your venture in, can be quite the asset for your startup, allowing you to avoid mistakes, utilize relationships, and build with insider knowledge.

Much of the advice is the same if you're a first-time founder but you're not a student. The downside is that many of the resources you'll need aren't teed up and curated for you like they are on many

6 Azoulay, P. , B. Jones, J. Kim, and J. Miranda. (2018). "Research: The Average Age of a Successful Startup Founder Is 45." *Harvard Business Review*. https://hbr.org/2018/07/research-the-average-age-of-a-successful-startup-founder-is-45

college campuses. Furthermore, you won't qualify for student discounts, grants, or free resources designed for students.

Regardless, you'll want to find a relevant community. The community should be a good fit for your business. The right fit may be related to the industry, resources offered, or stage of your business. These communities provide similar benefits to what we offer at The Garage: a community of entrepreneurial peers, mentorship, and resources like discounted professional services and a makerspace. Being part of one of these communities makes it easier to pull all the pieces together and to seek advice from friendly peers if you get stuck.

You may also want to consider an accelerator program when you're a little further along. Like everything, there are good, average, and bad accelerators. Look for a program that aligns with your business industry and stage. Do your homework and interview past participants to see if they would recommend the program for you.

We believe entrepreneurship is for everyone regardless of age. Younger founders have the advantages of fresh eyes, energy, and usually a better understanding of current trends and technologies. Starting younger also gives you a head start on building your entrepreneurial mindset and skill set, allowing you to get in some early reps, so you can make better use of the resources that will be provided to you as a college student. On the other hand, older founders have the advantage of experience, industry expertise, and robust professional networks and are more likely to succeed as founders. Regardless of your age, we encourage you as an aspiring founder to surround yourself with a community of like-minded, entrepreneurial people and to learn by doing.

KEY TAKEAWAYS

- Younger entrepreneurs can get a head start on building an entrepreneurial mindset and skill set earlier in life.
- Older entrepreneurs are more likely to be successful with their ventures.

SUMMARY OF PART I

W hew! That was a lot. It typically takes us many conversations over months or years to convey all of these ideas to student founders (along with them learning some of the lessons the hard way), and you just breezed right through it! Hopefully you've absorbed some of this information and have a better idea of the road ahead, the obstacles you'll inevitably face, and how you'll approach overcoming them. If so, you've got quite the head start!

Before we dive into part II, which has more focused, tactical steps and concepts (including idea evaluation, business models, customer acquisition channels, forming a business entity, and more), let's take a minute to recap what we've learned so far.

If you've made it this far, we're guessing you're well aware of the many benefits of entrepreneurship, but hopefully, you also understand that it's not an easy journey. You will face rejection and failure—a lot of it! But that is no reason to not try, and even "failure" isn't really failure. No matter your background or experiences, you can be an entrepreneur! Entrepreneurship is not limited to the twenty-year-old software engineer wunderkind building the next tech unicorn. Anyone who is creating something new in the world is an entrepreneur.

Trust yourself. Do the work. Forge your own path. Celebrate failure. These are our guiding principles at The Garage, and we hope you'll share them too.

When you have the spark of an idea that you may want to work on, take a Warm-Up Lap! Do a little bit of research to see if it is feasible or already exists. Get it out of your head and into a form you can share with someone else you trust to get their feedback. And be sure to do a gut check that you're still excited about the idea for the right reasons.

Hopefully, you now know that your initial idea probably isn't going to be your last idea, but by thinking like a scientist, you can test your assumptions, get feedback from customers, and iterate and improve your idea. Then run another experiment. And another. And remember to talk to customers *before* you spend too much time building your prototype.

The three biggest mistakes first-time founders make are (1) giving up too easily, (2) building something no one wants, and (3) ignoring distribution. You should already be inoculated to the first mistake, because you understand the journey won't be easy, and you have the tools and process to keep going. Talking to customers early and often, building an MVP, and thinking like a scientist will help you avoid building something no one wants. And remember to put considerable time and intention into figuring out your go-to-market plan or how you can efficiently get your product in front of customers.

Problem–solution fit and product–market fit are two important milestones that signal it's time for the next step in your journey. You've reached problem–solution fit once you know who your customer is, what problem you're solving for them, and that they find your solution valuable. This means it's time to focus on improving your current product for your customer, rather than going out to find more customers! Product–market fit is achieved when your customers are delighted and telling their friends about your product, and your biggest problem is keeping up with demand. At this point, it's time to scale your business and focus on growing your customer base!

Although our research of successful entrepreneurs—those who have founded a company and scaled it to millions of dollars in revenue—reveals some similarities in their high ambition and sociability and low prudence, this doesn't mean that you can't succeed without these traits. In fact, finding a cofounder with complementary skills and personality traits can be a huge asset! But don't rush into a cofounder relationship. Make sure you are aligned on your vision, priorities, desired outcomes, values, and how you work best together.

You are never too young to get started. You are never too old to get started. Just get started! And remember, storytelling is a super-power for entrepreneurs. Practicing and iterating your story to customers, to potential teammates, and even potentially to investors is imperative to your success. Finally, creating something new and putting it out in the world—aka being entrepreneurial—will become part of *your* story. It will unlock many doors and open up all kinds of opportunities you couldn't imagine. Even if one particular project doesn't succeed, you won't regret trying. And we'll be right here cheering you on!

Part II

USING YOUR SUPERPOWER

One of the first programs many students join at The Garage is our Tinker program, which helps students explore entrepreneurship at their own pace. Each week, students are sent an email on a relevant startup topic to help them explore their idea more deeply. The intention of these emails is to familiarize first-time student entrepreneurs with the concepts, vocabulary, and frameworks for launching a startup. Exposure to these concepts is paramount for success when starting a company, and having the knowledge and vocabulary to draw from makes the journey that much easier. These weekly emails typically range in reading time from five to ten minutes and are in no way meant to be definitive. Rather, we hope that students understand the basic ideas and frameworks and are better equipped to find further resources on the topics themselves, either through The Garage or the magic of the internet.

In part II, we'll share content from those emails. You can read and reflect on a chapter per week or you may choose to read it all at once. At the end of each chapter is a challenge, an activity for you to personalize the topic as it relates to your startup or entrepreneurial endeavor.

SO, YOU WANT TO START A STARTUP?

First, let's demystify what "starting a startup" really means. Many people think it's some herculean task that only people with extraordinary skills or intelligence can accomplish. But the truth is that it isn't rocket science (unless you're Elon Musk starting SpaceX). Paul Graham, the founder of Silicon Valley's Y Combinator accelerator program, which has been formative in the success of companies like Airbnb, Dropbox, DoorDash, Reddit, Twitch, and thousands of others, wrote an essay years ago titled

"How to Start a Startup." While the essay may be old, the sentiment is timeless. Here are a few excerpts:

> You need three things to create a successful startup: to start with good people, to make something customers actually want, and to spend as little money as possible. Most startups that fail do it because they fail at one of these. A startup that does all three will probably succeed. And that's kind of exciting, when you think about it, because all three are doable. Hard but doable. If there is one message I'd like to get across about startups, that's it. There is no magically difficult step that requires brilliance to solve.

> What you should do in college is work on your own projects. [People] should do this even if they don't plan to start startups, because it's the only real way to learn how to program. In some cases you may collaborate with other students, and this is the best way to get to know good [people]. The project may even grow into a startup. But once again, I wouldn't aim too directly at either target. Don't force things; just work on stuff you like with people you like.

If you want to do it, do it. Starting a startup is
not the great mystery it seems from outside. It's
not something you have to know about "business" to do. Build something users love, and
spend less than you make. How hard is that?

Pretty good advice, huh? So, let's say you've decided that you
want to be an entrepreneur. Where do you begin? The best place
to start is identifying a problem that people currently face and
creating a better solution to that problem. A "better solution"
could be a product or service that is easier to use, less expensive
(in time or money), or just a significantly better experience or
outcome for people.

But all problems aren't created equally. Some are minor incon-
veniences that only a few people face and aren't willing to pay for
solutions to, and others are significant, urgent, and affect millions
of people. One framework for evaluating startup ideas is identifying how big the problem you're solving actually is in the real world.

For example, is the problem you're solving—

- Popular? Many people face this problem.

- Urgent? When people face this problem, they need to solve
  it immediately.

- Growing? More and more people are facing this problem,
  or it's getting worse.

- Expensive? Current solutions to the problem cost people
  lots of time or money.

- Mandatory? There's no way around the problem for the people facing it.

- Frequent? Do people face this problem on a monthly, weekly, daily, or hourly basis?

Very few startups are tackling problems that have every single one of these characteristics. Very few, if any, companies are successful if the problem they're solving doesn't have at least one of these characteristics. If you're able to identify a problem that has multiple markers of being a big problem, you're off to a good start! You'll get a chance to try this in the challenge below.

While ideas are important, no startup or business has succeeded just because they had a good idea. In fact, having an idea is the easy part! Building an initial idea into something people are willing to pay for while spending less money than you earn is the difficult part. Your initial idea will probably change and morph into other forms as you get feedback from users and customers— and that's a good thing!

CHALLENGE

Write down twenty-five ideas for projects that would improve *something* for *someone*. You don't have to figure out how to make a business out of your solutions, just think of things that would solve a problem for someone, anyone! Your solutions could even be hypothetical (but let's avoid magic or violating the laws of physics)! If you're already working on a project or company, include it as one of your twenty-five ideas.

After you have twenty-five ideas, pick your top ten and rate them (popular, urgent, growing, expensive, mandatory, and frequent). Have you identified a handful of problems that have a couple of characteristics of being big? Think about how you might address solving these problems, and which ones excite you the most.

$\overbrace{(12)}$

CONDUCTING MARKET AND CUSTOMER RESEARCH

This stage includes both market research and customer research. Essentially, you want to become an expert on all other attempts to solve the problem and understand what potential customers value in a solution. Building a product before you learn about these two things could launch you down the wrong path, building something that already exists or that customers aren't interested in.

MARKET RESEARCH

Conducting market research practically just means a lot of googling. The most important thing you're searching for is every company or product in the market that could be competitive to your idea. The best way to do this is to act like a potential customer and search for the things they would probably search for. For instance, if you wanted to open a new pizza restaurant in Chicago, you might search for "pizza restaurant Chicago." Take note of the results and the details that might be important to how you build your idea to be different: their locations, price points, style of pizza, Yelp rating, and so on. Where are the gaps in the market or opportunities to offer a differentiated experience or product?

Here are a few market research questions to answer:

1. What are all of the current solutions/competitors?
   a. How much do they cost to use (time, money, etc.)?
   b. What is wrong or subpar about them? What could be improved?
2. How many people does this problem affect?
   a. Who are they (age, demographic, interests, etc.)?
3. Where are the opportunities to get in front of potential customers?
   a. Where do they spend their time (in person, online, community involvement, etc.)?
   b. Who/what do they trust (their friends, influencers, thought leaders, websites, ads)?

After conducting market research, you should be familiar with every company and product that could be a competitor to your idea, and know more about who and where your potential customers are. This will make it easier to build a product that is differentiated from others in the market and allow you to find and reach customers more efficiently.

CUSTOMER RESEARCH

Before you build anything, it's a good idea to actually talk to people who you think will be interested in your idea. The goal here is to validate that your idea or approach is something that customers would be willing to try.

A few common mistakes first-time founders make when conducting initial customer research include—

- Only talking to people who they know will be supportive, such as friends or family members
- Using a survey to collect responses instead of having a conversation with people

The reason surveys are problematic is that it is difficult to get people to complete them. They also typically lead to inconclusive data, and it is often impossible to follow up on interesting answers. Instead of surveys or talking to friends, reach out to a few people who are facing the problem you're trying to solve, and ask if they'd be open to a ten- to fifteen-minute conversation about it. We recommend having conversations with eight potential customers in your initial customer research phase, which should give you enough information and data to have a better understanding of what your product will need to address.

Here are five questions to ask potential customers, as recommended by Y Combinator's Startup School:

1. What's the hardest part about [doing this thing]?
2. Tell me about the last time you encountered this problem.
3. Why was that hard?
4. What, if anything, have you done to solve that problem?
5. What don't you love about the solutions you've tried?

Be sure to follow up on any interesting insights that someone reveals that you hadn't thought of! You can also ask if they'd be interested in trying your specific product, why or why not, and how much they'd be willing to pay (if anything) for your solution.

The information you collect should give you a better idea about what your customers want, where they're likely to search for your product, and how much they value a solution.

CHALLENGE

Have a short conversation with eight people who face the problem you are trying to solve, and record their responses. Identify the novel insights you had not thought of before your conversations and the commonalities between each person's answers to your questions. Use this information to formulate what your solution will need to entail to be attractive to the people you spoke with.

(13)

BUILDING YOUR MVP

The first version of your product is known as a *minimum viable product*, or MVP. You'll want to build an MVP to begin collecting customer feedback and making improvements.

The concept of an MVP was popularized in the book *The Lean Startup*, which helped launch a revolution in how startups thought about launching their first products. Instead of writing intricate business plans full of assumptions about what customers wanted and taking months or years to develop and release a "finished" product, the idea is to get feedback from customers as early as possible by releasing a simple version of your product and putting it in their hands. From the book—

The goal of a startup is to figure out the right thing to build—the thing customers want and will pay for—as quickly as possible.

The fundamental activity of a startup is to turn ideas into products (build), measure how customers respond (measure), and then learn whether to pivot or persevere (learn). This is known as the *build–measure–learn feedback loop*. All successful startup processes should be geared to accelerate that feedback loop.

What differentiates the success stories from the failures is that the successful entrepreneurs had the foresight, the ability, and the tools to discover which parts of their plans were working brilliantly and which were misguided and [to] adapt their strategies accordingly.[7]

In other words, to find out what customers really want, it's better to give them an early version of your product vision, measure how they interact with it, and ask them for feedback directly than to build out your final product vision before launch. After all, what if it turns out the customer doesn't actually want the product you're building? It's better to learn that sooner rather than later.

---

7   Ries, E. (2001). *The Lean Startup*. VIKIN.

For example, an early version of the Airbnb website did not have map view available. It also did not have payments integrated and was built by a part-time CTO. Still, the company was able to gauge interest from users and collect feedback on what features were most important to them. Airbnb was therefore utilizing the build–measure–learn feedback loop from the very beginning.

Your MVP should be a version of your product with just enough features to satisfy early customers and provide feedback for future product development. The functionality should be clear to the user (they know exactly what you're offering), and it should be easy and intuitive to use. How will you know if this is the case? You'll ask them!

Using the input you get back from customers, you can revise your assumptions, redesign your product or offering, add features, and make small adjustments (iterations) or large adjustments (pivots) to better accommodate your early adopters.

CHALLENGE

Build an MVP of your product and release it to potential customers! This could be a simple website landing page that explains your product and allows them to sign up for updates, a duct-taped-together physical product, or any other way you can communicate your product vision to potential customers and begin providing value to them. Send this version to the respondents from your customer research survey from last week, and see what they think!

PROTECTING YOUR INTELLECTUAL PROPERTY AND CREATING A BUSINESS ENTITY

Student founders are often excited to work on building their idea and less excited to do paperwork and navigate legal agreements. This chapter could have easily been called "things you need to talk to an attorney about." However, getting this part of your business right is as important as getting your product or service right. In this chapter, we'll share our opinion on these topics and try to simplify them as much as possible, but as with anything having to do with the law, we encourage you to speak with an attorney. For this section, we took our own advice and consulted with Patrick Richards, a partner at the law firm K&L Gates LLP, who has worked with many of our student founders.

INTELLECTUAL PROPERTY

Intellectual property, or IP for short, is a legal term referring to the ownership of an idea, design, or invention by the person who came up with it.

There are four types of intellectual property:

1. **Trademarks**: names, logos, and taglines that identify your brand

2. **Patents**: new and useful inventions

3. **Copyrights**: original works of authorship, including writings, music, art, photographs, and videos

4. **Trade secrets**: valuable confidential information

A well-crafted IP strategy focuses on building value in your brand by using protection for your unique selling propositions to differentiate your products and services in the marketplace. Generally speaking, businesses do this by using the competitive advantage provided by their patents, copyrights, and trade secrets to build value in their trademarks. We recognize Disney as a valuable entertainment company whose trademark is valuable because of the value of its movies' copyrights. The trademarks in pharmaceutical brands, like Tylenol, were built on the value of their patented drugs. Coca-Cola's trademarks are strengthened by the trade secret that protects the Coke recipe.

What follows is a brief introduction to each IP regime to help you think about how IP rights might affect your business. It may also help you open a conversation about IP rights with your mentors and lawyers. You can use these introductions to help you start thinking about how to best use your patents, copyrights, and trade secrets to build more valuable trademarks.

Trademarks

Trademarks are the names, logos, and taglines that identify your business to your customers. It's important to take a thoughtful approach to your trademarks early, as missteps can be costly and require you to rebrand your business just as you begin to gain traction in the market. A worst-case scenario is that you spend a lot of time and money building a company brand only to find out that you have to change your name, because someone else already owns the trademark. For this reason, it's important to address potential trademarks at an early stage.

There are two main considerations with trademarks:

1. Is your mark confusingly similar to rights already owned by a third party?

2. Is your mark appropriately distinctive such that the US Patent and Trademark Office (USPTO) will grant you enforceable rights?

These are questions best addressed by a trademark attorney. However, at the earliest stages, particularly as you start narrowing down the name of the business or product, it can be helpful to use the USPTO trademark search tools (https://www.uspto.gov /trademarks/search) to help focus your initial name selection. These tips for using the USPTO search tools can help you perform more useful searches, particularly to find names that clearly are not available. It is also important to use Google to see if you can find any conflicting uses of the trademark by other companies. Trademark rights do not need to be registered at the USPTO to be enforceable, so there is definitely value in looking for unregistered uses.

Once you start narrowing down the list of potential trademarks to a few favorites, it is best to meet with a trademark attorney to help determine the relative strengths and risks of each so you can make an informed decision before putting real investment into building your brand.

Trademarks can be registered at the federal or state level, but trademarks are not required to be registered to be enforceable. As soon as a brand begins selling goods or services using a trademark, the company develops common law rights in that mark in the territory where it's being used. Unregistered marks can be designated using a superscript TM, such as MyBrand™. Once a mark

is federally registered, it can use the circle R, such as MyBrand°.
Although you start developing rights in unregistered marks simply through their use, registered marks have many advantages
over unregistered marks and are definitely worth exploring with
proper guidance. Registered marks provide greater protection and
are significantly more likely to be upheld in court than unregistered marks. For example, registered marks have legal priority
across the United States, even in a territory in which the mark is
not already being used.

At a minimum, you should check the USPTO and Google for
potential trademark issues with the name you've picked for your
company. It is important that you choose a mark that does not
infringe upon third-party rights and ensure it is something that
you can build value in over time. If you have the resources to do so,
you should also meet with a trademark attorney when you develop
a new name or logo for a business, product, or service. The cost
for registering a trademark will vary based on the legal service provider you use and the complexity of the mark itself. However, the
typical startup should budget $2,000–$3,000 for comprehensive
trademark representation in its first year.

Patents

Patents protect inventions from being copied by competitors.
However, although we might think the term *inventions* is fairly
broad, the patent system has limitations on what qualifies for
patent protection and what does not. While there are exceptions

in both directions, inventions in the pharmaceutical and life sciences spaces, medical devices, and other mechanical and electrical hardware devices are more likely to be patentable. Most projects directed to websites, apps, software, and service companies will have a much harder time finding patentable inventions and, as a result, very often should not concern themselves with the time and cost involved in applying for a patent.

There are different types of patents, and within each type of patent, there are varying levels of complexity. Depending on your invention and the type of patent, the initial steps of applying for a patent will typically cost between $5,000 and $15,000+, including fees for patent searches, application fees, illustrations, and attorney fees. To go from start to finish in the patent process can take several years and can be many tens of thousands of dollars, depending on how difficult of an examination the patent undergoes. Accordingly, even though it may be valuable to speak with a patent attorney to assess the potential value in pursuing patent protection for your invention, just because you can file a patent application doesn't mean you should file a patent application. Before making the investment, there should be a very clear business purpose for pursuing a patent.

Any time you invent a new product that you believe didn't previously exist, you will want to assess the likelihood that it can be patented. Similarly, any time you are bringing a new product to market, you will want to assess the likelihood that it infringes third-party patents. The best way to do this is to speak to a patent attorney.

Copyrights

Copyrights are a form of protection provided to the authors of "original works of authorship fixed in tangible media." Copyright protection is acquired simply by fixing your original work of authorship in some tangible form. What that means is that, if you think of an original story and tell it to those around you, you do not have material covered by copyright protection. However, by simply writing your story down or by making a recording of yourself telling the story, you have acquired copyright protection. Like trademarks, although some rights naturally result from the creation of the copyright material, federal registration can help to strengthen and perfect those rights.

Copyrights are typically thought of as covering literary works, performing and musical arts, visual arts, motion pictures, photographs, and other artistic works. But copyright protection also extends to computer programs, data sets, blogs, and websites. And, as with patents and trademarks, we aren't merely interested in protecting what's ours. It is just as important to make sure you aren't infringing upon the rights of others.

It is uncommon for student projects at The Garage to need to actively register copyrights at an early stage of the business. However, it is more common that these student projects could benefit from better understanding whether their business plan requires the use (and licensing) of any third-party copyrights.

It's important to think through whether you have any potential copyright infringement issues to consider. For example, does your business require the use of someone else's software? Are you planning to use someone else's compilation of data? Are you planning to use someone else's videos or photographs?

Another copyright consideration is whether you have the appropriate agreements in place so the people creating content for your business (taking photos, writing content, recording music, etc.) have assigned their rights to the business. If not, you might run into a situation where someone you thought was creating content for your business actually owns that content.

Although it is uncommon for an early-stage startup to need to budget for filing copyright protection, talking through copyright issues with an IP lawyer may help you identify licenses, service agreements, and other business concerns that need to be addressed. Consider speaking with an attorney any time your business plans to make commercial use of original content or of third-party content, to assess whether there are any copyright ownership/licensing issues.

Trade secrets

Trade secrets are confidential information that provides your business a competitive advantage. Unlike trademarks, patents, and copyrights, there is no registration procedure for trade secrets. You protect trade secrets simply by keeping them secret.

When assessing what information your business may have that can be protected as a trade secret, you should consider how easy the information will be to reverse engineer by your competitors. Some products and services, by their very nature, reveal exactly what they are to anyone that uses them. Other products and services are less revealing. For example, although anyone that uses Google to search for content online understands that there is a search algorithm that ranks the online content in response to a search inquiry, the actual algorithm cannot easily be reverse engineered. Keeping the algorithm secret protects its value from competitors.

Once you have identified whether your business has any proprietary information that should be protected as a trade secret, you will want to take steps to keep the information confidential by limiting access to it to the smallest number of people necessary and by having those with access to it sign nondisclosure and confidentiality agreements. While neither complex nor costly, trade secrets can be very important, and, for that reason, it is worth taking some time to talk through your potential trade secrets with an IP attorney.

CREATING A BUSINESS ENTITY

When your idea moves from an idea or project to a business, you need to form a legal business entity. You will need to form a business entity to do everything from opening a business bank account to hiring a freelancer. Most importantly, forming a business entity gives you certain legal rights, protections, and opportunities. For example, this often means you can't be held personally liable for the company's legal and financial problems. If someone spills hot coffee in their lap at your coffee shop, they can sue the business, but they can't sue you personally.

Don't worry! While this may sound like a big deal, it's pretty easy to do. In our opinion, most student founders should form an LLC in their state of residence. In Illinois, at the time of publishing, registering an Illinois LLC online with the secretary of state takes about fifteen minutes and a $150 filing fee. There is an ongoing annual fee of $75, and if you need to close the business, there is a $5 fee.

Students often wonder when they should form a business entity. There's a little bit of a gray area, but some of the most common trigger events include signing a contract on behalf of your startup, selling a product or service (i.e., when you start to earn money), incurring any meaningful expenditures (i.e., buying equipment or leasing a retail space), hiring a contractor or employee, and taking any action that may create liability (i.e., you'll want to get business liability insurance before, say, opening a trampoline business).

LLCs have two different possible management structures: manager managed and member managed. In a member-managed LLC, all of the members (owners) participate in managing the business. In a manager-managed LLC, only designated members are given the responsibility to run the business. We recommend a manager-managed LLC and that one cofounder takes on this responsibility. This is usually the person with the CEO or COO title or whoever is the most detail oriented and enjoys paperwork. Delegating management to one person can ensure smoother management of the business. However, each situation is different, and you will need to decide what's best for your business.

One field that is always on the entity formation paperwork is your business name. While you can change this later if needed (for a fee, of course), it's nice to get this right the first time. Hopefully, you followed our advice in the trademarks section and have found a name that you like, that is available, and that does not infringe upon third-party rights.

Depending on the entity type you choose, you'll also need to draft a document called *articles of organization*. Depending on your state and entity type, this document can also be called an *article of incorporation*, a *certificate of organization*, or a *certificate of formation*. Simply put, this is a legal document that outlines how you're going to run your business. Each state has its articles of organization form available online via the appropriate state agency website. There may be some overlap between your founders' agreement and your articles of organization. Your founders' agreement is an internal document, while your articles of organization must be shared and filed with the state in which you are registering.

Registering your LLC and submitting your articles of organization will allow your company to operate legally. Afterward, your startup can get an employee identification number from the Internal Revenue Service (IRS) and obtain a federal tax ID number. This will allow you to do things like open a bank account, get a business banking credit card, pay a contractor, or hire an employee. In other words, all the things you need to conduct business!

Another consideration at this point is business insurance. Business insurance protects you when and if bad things happen. For example, if an employee crashes a company-owned car, a customer gets hurt using your product or visiting your retail location, or an unhappy client sues you. Business insurance can be complex for a novice. We recommend asking for a recommendation to a broker that specializes in business insurance to help you through the process.

The two other common business entities we see at The Garage are Delaware C corporations and 501(c)3 nonprofit corporations. In our opinion, you should only create a Delaware C corporation if you know you will be raising venture capital. It is very rare for a student founder to know this, and a C corporation is a more complex entity type to manage. If your startup does get traction and you do need to raise venture capital, your investors will require you to convert to a Delaware C corporation, and you can work with an attorney to convert from an LLC to a C corporation.

A 501(c)3 nonprofit corporation is for charitable organizations that qualify for federal tax exemption, under—you guessed it—section 501(c)3 of the United States tax code. Nonprofit organizations should follow the application process on the IRS website. 501(c)3s are relatively complex entities to set up and manage, so we recommend finding a mentor with experience running and operating a nonprofit to help you with this.

A caveat for international students: Forming a legal business entity can conflict with your student visa status. In a worst-case scenario, this could mean voiding your student visa and getting deported. Each visa situation is unique, so we recommend that international students consult with an attorney who specializes in immigration before registering a legal business entity.

Intellectual property and entity formation can be complex, but the good news is there are professionals who specialize in each of these topics that can help and guide you. Educate yourself by reading up on these subjects online. If possible, meet with an attorney or expert for free that provides office hours on your campus or in your local startup community. You can also talk with other entrepreneurs who are a few steps ahead of you.

CHALLENGE

Do a USPTO and Google search for five potential business names and look for any existing businesses with similar names to the one you have chosen. You may also want to research website URLs and social media handles for each name. And if your preferred names are taken, pick another one and search again. Get creative!

IDENTIFYING YOUR BUSINESS PLAN AND BUSINESS MODEL

I f your company is going to be successful and ultimately profitable and sustainable, you'll need to find the business models that align your interests with your customers'. There are three major categories of business models: those whose revenue primarily comes from other businesses, known as business-to-business (B2B); those whose revenue primarily comes from consumers, known as business-to-consumer (B2C); and those whose revenue primarily comes from intermediary businesses, who ultimately sell to consumers, known as business-to-business-to-consumer (B2B2C). Some companies will stick to one model, and others will utilize a blended approach.

POTENTIAL REVENUE STREAMS

Now, let's dive deeper into revenue streams. Simply put, how does your company make money? Following is a list of some popular revenue streams to consider. Each revenue stream has its pros and cons and is ideal for different types of products and customers. It's also possible to combine multiple revenue streams in your business, such as monetizing through a monthly subscription and advertising.

Transactional

Customers buy your product once for a fixed price. This could be a physical or digital good or service, but the customer is only paying once for a specific product.

- Examples: iPhones, clothes and apparel, pizza

- Pros: It's easy to figure out how much customers value your product (the price they're willing to pay).

- Cons: Your pricing must be high enough to ensure you make a profit on every sale, including the marketing costs to acquire the customer, because you don't know if those customers will return and purchase again. In the long run, it's important to expand your product line, so you have more opportunities to monetize your customers.

Subscription/membership

Customers pay for access to your product or service on a recurring basis.

- Examples: Netflix, Headspace, Birchbox

- Pros: Subscription revenue streams can be easier to manage, because you're equipped with more data to understand your customers and what they value in your product. If your pricing is right, it can be easier to make a profit on each customer over time, if they remain subscribed.

- Cons: Once customers unsubscribe (also called *churn*), it's very difficult to get them to return, and new subscribers are often more expensive to acquire. It's important that customers continuously see the value in their subscription.

Advertising

A company offers a free service to consumers and derives revenue entirely, or predominantly, from advertisers or sponsors. Common advertising companies include social networks and content sites.

- Examples: Instagram, TikTok, Morning Brew newsletter

- Pros: If you can build a big enough audience and launch an advertising product that performs well for your customers (advertisers, *not* users), ad-supported businesses can be very profitable while remaining free for your end users.

- Cons: Ad-supported business models are incredibly difficult to start from scratch. You must (1) build a large enough audience to be attractive to advertisers; (2) conduct difficult and time-consuming ad-sales efforts to companies, agencies, and brands; and (3) be able to report on the ROI and effectiveness of their campaigns to justify them continuing to use your platform. Most of this is a completely separate focus from building your product for end users and can also be in conflict with their user experience.

Marketplaces

Act as an intermediary in the sale of a good or service between sellers and buyers, generally collecting a percentage of the total transaction value.

- Examples: Etsy, eBay, Cameo

- Pros: Marketplaces can unlock pent-up supply and demand for people who are willing to do business together but otherwise wouldn't be connected. They're therefore willing to pay you a significant fee to facilitate these connections and transactions.

- Cons: Marketplaces are difficult to get started because of the chicken-or-the-egg problem: Do you start with supply (sellers) or demand (buyers)? It's difficult to prove the value of your marketplace to one side before the other side is already there and willing to transact.

Usage-based fee

Customers pay more for your product or service the more they use it. This model is most often used for B2B software-based products.

- Examples: Metromile, Amazon Web Services, Google Maps API

- Pros: This pricing model aligns the incentives of the customer and company well, as you pay more as you use more (and vice versa).

- Cons: It can be difficult to figure out pricing for users of different magnitudes.

- Again, this isn't an exhaustive list of the ways your customers may pay for your product, but it's a good starting point to think about.

CHALLENGE

Take some time to think about how your company could utilize each of these revenue streams. What would a subscription model look like? How about ad support? For each model, write down the pros and cons specifically with your business and customers. Is there one clear revenue stream that aligns your interests with your customers'? If so, ask some potential customers and/or users what they think about that offering.

GETTING CUSTOMERS

By this point, you've found a problem that people face that is worth solving, researched the market and competition for your solution, built and launched an MVP, and received feedback from your first customers, or early adopters. Today, we're going to talk about where to find your first 10, 100, and 1,000 customers. Of course, this will depend on your specific product and customers, but there are many acquisition channels to consider and test.

Julia Enthoven, the founder of cloud-based editing software startup Kapwing, in San Francisco, has written a couple of great articles about how her company got their first ten paying customers in two weeks and why you shouldn't pay to acquire your first users. The general concept for early-stage startups is that to find your early adopters, you should do things that don't scale. What this means is that you want to put extra effort to get in front of your target customers organically (without paying for ads), even if that means putting flyers across campus, which wouldn't be a scalable way to acquire thousands or millions of new customers. Julia explains:

> The best products elegantly solve someone's desperate need. Finding that need and the people who have it is a challenging but essential process for entrepreneurs. Don't cheat yourself of these learnings by buying your first customers. Instead, embrace the hustle and find ways to sell, distribute, and persuade without cash.[8]

By earning your first customers without spending money on advertising, you are not only saving money for your company but also collecting valuable learnings about where to reach more potential customers and what acquisition channels work best for your product. At a high level, there are two categories of marketing: organic and paid.

ORGANIC MARKETING

The goal of organic marketing is to get your product in front of people without spending any money. Most of these strategies are

---

8 Enthoven, J. (2019). "Don't Pay to Acquire Your First Users." Kapwing Company Blog. https://www.kapwing.com/blog/dont-pay-to-acquire-your-first-users

worth pursuing for the life of your company, even once you start using paid marketing as well.

Word of mouth

The gold standard of customer acquisition is word-of-mouth recommendations from your current customers. People are much more likely to try a new product if their friends recommend it, so building a product good enough for your customers to tell their friends about it should be your North Star.

Search engine optimization (SEO)

SEO means being a top organic result (not an ad!) when someone googles the problem that your product solves. This strategy is complex and takes time to build but is worth pursuing in the long run.

Earned media/press

Any time your company is featured in an article or you're interviewed by a publication or on a podcast, this is known as *earned media*, because you earned the attention of the interviewer, who helps share your story with their audience (completely free!). You can reach out to journalists, publications, and podcasters to pitch your product or yourself as a story that may be interesting to them. The best strategy is to focus on the media outlets that your target customers are also customers of.

Content marketing

You can write, publish, and distribute articles or case studies about your product or problem that you're solving to establish yourself as an expert and build an audience who may one day convert into customers. Both Glossier and Goop began as blogs—not businesses!

Organic social media

Find where your customers are on Twitter, Instagram, Reddit, TikTok, and other social media channels, and interact with them directly, evangelizing with an authentic voice about why they should try your product.

Cold email/outreach

If you can find their information, email or message people who you think would be interested in trying out your product.

In-person sales

If your product is for members of a fraternity, visit fraternities, and tell their members about your product. If your product is for senior citizens, visit retirement homes to meet senior citizens. In-person sales simply means going to the physical places that your customers are and talking to them directly about your product.

Flyers

Putting flyers around campus is another example of organic marketing!

PAID MARKETING

Paid marketing is useful to reach customers once you know more about them and your current customers are satisfied with your product. While you may be able to acquire new customers in paid marketing channels relatively inexpensively at the beginning, these channels inevitably get more expensive as you spend more, since you pick the low-hanging fruit first. Therefore, spending too much in any channel before you know your customers are satisfied can be an expensive mistake.

Referral programs

You can offer your current customers a discount if they recruit their friends to become your customers as well. While you may not be "paying" out of pocket for these customers, offering them a discounted rate is a form of paying.

Google ads

Search engine marketing is when you purchase ads to appear in the results for specific searches.

Paid social media

These channels allow you to target users based on their interests, demographics, and location, among other things. While their ad formats and products differ slightly, each site does a good job of walking new advertisers through best practices. Be sure to check out paid social options on Facebook, Instagram, Snapchat, Twitter, TikTok, YouTube, Pinterest, Reddit, and LinkedIn.

Blogs

Offer bloggers (especially ones your customers read) a discount or free version of your product if they feature your product in one of their posts. Make sure they link back to your company's website, since this helps with your SEO.

Influencers

You can pay social media influencers to directly promote your product in a post. You can reach out to them directly or use an influencer platform to automate the process.

Traditional media

You can also use print (magazine and newspaper ads), out-of-home advertising (billboards, bus stop ads), radio or podcast advertisements, and television ads. Many of these mediums require more expensive, up-front ad buys and have less targeting capabilities, but they may make sense at a certain stage for your company.

It's important to note that successful companies will use many of these marketing channels and may use different channels at different points in the company's life cycle. You should be willing to constantly experiment with marketing channels to find the most efficient ways to acquire new customers.

CHALLENGE

Test five different customer acquisition channels, either from this chapter or others. For paid marketing channels, you don't have to spend much. ($25 is fine to experiment with!) The goal here is to find which channels are most effective and cost-efficient for acquiring your customers at the moment.

(17)

UNDERSTANDING HOW YOUR BUSINESS WORKS

When running a business, you have to know how your business works. You'll need to be thinking about things like how much it costs to acquire a new customer and how much profit an incremental sale will bring you. Knowing your metrics, both financial and customer-centric, allows you to optimize your business by finding room for improvement. In addition to building a stronger business, if you ever decide to raise money from someone else to fund your business (e.g., angel investors, venture capitalists), they'll expect you to provide these metrics and key performance indicators.

Following are some important metrics that you should be tracking. Not all of these apply to every business, but they are all worth understanding. This is not a comprehensive list, but it should give you an idea of the kinds of things you should be thinking about and optimizing for.

FINANCIAL METRICS

Revenue

This is the total amount of money your company brings in from normal business operations, including discounts and deductions for returned merchandise.

Cost of goods sold (COGS)

This is the direct cost of producing the goods sold by your company, including the cost of the materials and labor directly used to create the product.

Gross income/gross profit

This is the total revenue minus the COGS. If your gross income is positive, your product is profitable on a per-unit basis.

Gross profit margin is expressed as a percentage, a measure of profitability that shows the percentage of revenue that exceeds the COGS. You calculate it by dividing the difference between your revenue and COGS by your revenue. For example, if you sell a product for $100, and your COGS are $50, your gross profit margin would be 50% ($50/$100).

Net income/net profit

This is the total revenue minus COGS, expenses, depreciation and amortization, interest, and taxes. If your net income is positive, your company is profitable.

Net profit margin is expressed as a percentage, a measure of profitability that shows the percentage of revenue that exceeds all of your expenses. You calculate it by dividing your profit after all of your company expenses by your revenue. For example, if you sell one product for $100, your COGS are $50, and you spend $25 on marketing, administrative, and taxes, your net profit margin would be 25% ($25/$100).

Income Statement	
Revenue	$10,000
Cost of Goods Sold (COGS)	$4,000
Gross Income	$6,000
Expenses	
Marketing & Promotions	$1,000
General & Administrative	$2,000
Total Expenses	$3,000
Earnings Before Tax	$3,000
Taxes	$630
Net Income	$2,370

In the example in the table, the gross profit margin is 60% ($6,000/$10,000), and the net profit margin is 23.7% ($2,370/$10,000). The difference is that net income also includes all additional expenses of running your business, such as marketing and promotions, general and administrative expenses, depreciation, interest, and taxes.

Cash flow

This is the net amount of cash that an entity receives and disburses during a period of time. If you receive more cash in a given period than you disperse, you have positive cash flow, which makes financing your business easier.

Growth rate

This is the percentage change of a specific variable within a specific time period, typically revenue. Usually, this is used in an annual or monthly time period. You calculate it by subtracting your revenue in time period 1 from your revenue in time period 2 and dividing that result by the revenue in time period 1. For example, if your company had $10,000 of revenue in year 1 and $20,000 of revenue in year 2, you saw a 100% annual growth rate. ($20,000 – $10,000)/$10,000 = 1 or 100%.

Average order value (AOV)

This is the average dollar amount spent each time a customer places an order. You calculate it by dividing the total revenue by the number of orders. For example, if you had $1,000 in revenue from ten orders in one month, your AOV would be $100 ($1,000/10).

Burn

This is how much money your business is losing each month. Calculate it by subtracting the amount of money that goes out from the amount that comes in. For example, if, in one month, you brought in $1,000 in revenue but had $2,000 in expenses, your burn is $1,000.

Runway

This is how many months of cash you have left at your current burn rate. Take your current bank balance and divide it by your monthly burn. For example, if you have $10,000 in the bank and a monthly burn rate of $1,000, you have a ten-month runway ($10,000/$1,000).

Subscription businesses

Subscription-based services, which rely on recurring revenue, have additional metrics specific to this business model.

Recurring revenue

This is income earned on a recurring basis, such as subscriptions or memberships, which are often recurring monthly or yearly.

Your monthly recurring revenue (MRR) is the amount of revenue that recurs each month. For example, if you have 100 subscribers paying $10 per month, your MRR is $1,000.

Your annual run rate (ARR) is an extrapolation of your current MRR. Assuming nothing changes in the year ahead (no new subscribers, no churned customers), it will be the amount of revenue expected in one year. You calculate it by multiplying your MRR by 12 months; in the previous example, your ARR would be $12,000 ($1,000 × 12). Be careful not to confuse annual run rate with annual recurring revenue (also abbreviated as ARR), which is your actual annual recurring revenue as opposed to extrapolated current MRR over twelve months.

Revenue retention

This is the percentage of revenue from a cohort of customers that remained in a consecutive time period (month or year). Take the total revenue from your customers in the current month who were also customers in the previous month and divide by the total revenue from all customers in the prior month. For example, if, last month, your customers paid you $100 in total, and, this month, that same group of customers paid you $90, you'd have 90% revenue retention.

Physical products

Startups that produce or sell a physical product have different metrics from digital-based businesses. In particular, you will need to create a bill of materials. This is an extensive list of raw materials, components, and assemblies required to construct, manufacture, or repair a product or service. It includes product codes, part descriptions, quantities, costs, and additional specifications.

Marketplace businesses

Marketplace startups, which connect buyers and sellers, look at two additional metrics.

Gross merchandise volume (GMV)

This is the total sales dollar volume of merchandise transacting through the marketplace in a specific period. For example, if all Airbnb customers spend $1 billion on rentals in a month, the GMV is $1 billion. Note: This does not mean Airbnb's revenue was $1 billion. Most of the transaction volume is transferred to hosts.

Net revenue

This is the portion of GMV the company recognizes as revenue for services rendered. Using the previous example, if Airbnb charges a 10% fee on rentals, the company's net revenue on $1 billion of GMV would be $100 million ($1 billion × 10%).

CUSTOMER METRICS

Beyond measuring financial performance, you'll also need metrics to determine how well you are acquiring and retaining customers.

Customer acquisition cost (CAC)/blended CAC

This is how much it costs you to earn a new customer, including sales and marketing spend. This is known as *blended CAC* because it blends all of your customers, whether you earned them organically (free) or spent money on marketing or advertisements to acquire them. To calculate it, take your total sales and marketing spend and divide by the number of new customers in a time period. For example, if you spent $100 and acquired ten new customers, your CAC is $10.

Paid CAC

This is how much it costs you to earn a new customer, excluding organic customers. This will naturally be higher than your blended CAC, as you're excluding customers you spent $0 to acquire. For example, if you spent $100 and acquired four new customers through paid channels and six new customers organically, your paid CAC would be $25 ($100/4 new customers through paid channels).

You should also break down your paid CAC by channel and campaign to understand which are your most efficient (inexpensive) marketing channels. For example, Facebook CAC = $10, Instagram CAC = $9, Google CAC = $13, and so on.

Average revenue per user (ARPU)

This is just as it sounds. ARPU is the average revenue per user in a given time period, usually a month or year. To calculate it, divide your total revenue by the number of users in a given time period. For example, if you bring in $1,000 in revenue in a month that averaged 100 customers/users, your monthly ARPU is $10 ($1,000/100).

Payback period

This is the amount of time it takes for your company to recover the cost of acquiring one customer. It's calculated by dividing CAC by (ARPU × gross margin). For example, if your CAC is $8, your ARPU is $5, and your gross margin is 80%, your payback period is $8 CAC/($5 × 80%) = 2 months. A desirable benchmark is, generally, a payback period of less than five months.

Churn

This is the percentage of customers or users that stop using your product in a subsequent time period. Take your total lost customers (canceled subscriptions) in a given period and divide by the total number of customers in the prior period. For example, if you have 100 users in year 1, but only 80 of those users remain in year 2, you have 20% annual churn.

The best companies keep churn under 5% per year, which translates to 0.42% per month. This is a very difficult benchmark to meet, but it's worth optimizing for! It's generally easier to keep customers you already earned than acquire new customers.

User retention

User retention is the inverse of churn. It is the percentage of users who remain customers in a subsequent time period. In the previous example, there was 80% user retention, year over year.

Lifetime value (LTV)

This is an estimate of the average revenue that a customer will generate throughout their lifespan as a customer. Different types of businesses have different ways of calculating LTV, with subscription models being the most straightforward. In that case, simply take the ARPU and divide it by your churn rate. For example, if you charge $500 per month, and your churn rate is 5%, then your LTV for a new customer is $500/0.05 or $10,000.

For a nonsubscription model, multiply your AOV (the average order value) by the number of expected purchases and the time of engagement. The LTV of a customer can grow or shrink over time, based on your offerings and your ability to grow the account.

LTV:CAC ratio

This is a measure of how valuable new customers are compared to how expensive they are to acquire. For example, if your CAC is $20, and your LTV is $40, your LTV:CAC ratio is 2:1 ($40:$20).

You should aim to have an LTV:CAC ratio of at least 3:1. That is, a new customer will bring you three times more in incremental revenue than it costs to acquire them.

Active users

This is the total number of users or customers in a given period of time. These can be expressed in daily or monthly active users.

Conversion rate

This is the percentage of users who take a desired action. This is the percentage of visitors to your website who make a purchase. The *average* e-commerce conversion rate is between 2.5% and 3%.

Click-through rate (CTR)

In digital advertising, this the percentage of people who click a particular advertisement or hyperlink. The *average* click-through rate for advertisements on search platforms (e.g., Google) is around 2%. If your ads aren't performing above this CTR, you'll want to adjust them.

Organic vs. paid users

This is the split of your customers who you earned organically vs. the ones you used paid marketing channels to acquire. Generally, the higher percentage you can earn organically, the more desirable it is.

CHALLENGE

Figure out the metrics in this chapter that will apply to your business, and create a simple spreadsheet to track each of them every week and again at the end of each month. With this, you can begin to track your progress and improve your metrics to build a stronger business. Eventually, you'll want to upgrade your spreadsheet to an automated software product, but in the beginning, a simple spreadsheet on Google Sheets or Excel will suffice.

$$\left(18\right)$$

KNOWING WHEN TO PIVOT

Once your business starts acquiring customers, one of two things will likely happen: (1) Your customers will love your product, will continue being customers, and will promote your product to their friends! Acquiring new customers will seem easy, and your customers will be highly satisfied! (2) Or, more commonly, many of your customers won't return and won't tell their friends about your product. You'll find it difficult to acquire new customers, and those you have acquired won't love your product. In the second scenario, it may be time to pivot your product, strategy, or offering until you move toward the first scenario.

PIVOTING

The concept of pivoting has become popular with startups over the past few years, but pivoting really just means changing your idea. Often, startup ideas don't work as well as you may have originally imagined, but it's important to keep an open mind and be willing to change your strategy instead of continuing down a dead end.

Some of the most successful companies were once chasing entirely different ideas before pivoting. Did you know that Slack was originally producing an online multiplayer video game that wasn't finding success, before pivoting to sell the internal messaging tool they had developed in-house for their engineers to communicate? Or that Twitch, the video-game streaming website acquired for $970 million by Amazon, was originally called "Justin. TV" and was just a 24/7 livestream of cofounder Justin Kan's life? These founders were able to recognize that, while their original idea was not taking off, they had built something valuable, and if they found it valuable, perhaps other people would too.

When and why to pivot?

There will be times when you will need to pivot. Here are some examples:

- You have launched and have been trying to get users for weeks or months, but it feels hopeless.

- Your customers don't like your product after trying it, don't return, and don't tell their friends about it.

- You have little to no organic growth; you're fully reliant on paid marketing channels for customer acquisition.

- The idea is impossible to get started because it takes years to build or you need too much capital to get started.

- You know in your heart that it's not going to work.

- It's not growing.

- You don't enjoy working on it anymore.

- You're not a good fit to be working on the idea.

- You're relying on external factors outside of your control to make your startup take off.

- You're out of ideas on what to do differently to make your startup work.

Reasons people take too long to pivot

Sometimes pivoting can be challenging. There are many reasons people drag their heels on it. Here are some examples:

- Fear of admitting failure

- Aversion to loss

- Some traction and assume it will continue to grow

- Blame others for why it's not working: customers, investors, etc.

- A belief that "if you just believe hard enough, things will work out"

How to find a better idea

Sometimes, you'll need to keep searching for a better idea. Here are some tips:

- Look for something you are more excited about that makes you feel inspired to work on it.

- Identify something ancillary to your idea that you've built and find valuable/useful (e.g., Slack/Twitch).

- Make an honest assessment of your strengths/weaknesses, and attempt to find something with better founder–market fit.

- Try lots of small things that are easy to test and to get market feedback on.

Knowing when to pivot is a delicate balance. Founders incapable of changing ideas struggle, and founders who change ideas too often also struggle. Find the happy medium. Changing your idea based on market feedback is an important part of building a startup. The goal at this stage of your company is to find product–market fit.

PRODUCT–MARKET FIT

The concept of product–market fit was developed by Andy Rachleff, the founder and former CEO of Wealthfront and cofounder of storied venture capital firm Benchmark Capital. While there are many different descriptions of product–market fit, perhaps the most straightforward is that you know you have product–market fit when growth is not your biggest problem; keeping up with demand is. This means you have strong organic growth (people are talking about your product), your customers are happy (they're returning and are happy), and you have to dedicate more resources to keep up with demand—whether that be manufacturing more product, scaling up your cloud-server provider, or hiring more team members to service additional customers.

CHALLENGE

It's important not to become married to your original idea and to be open to pivoting. Whether or not you are currently at a point to evaluate whether you should pivot, take some time to brainstorm ten alternative approaches or ideas based on everything that you have learned from your experience so far with research, building an MVP, marketing, and customer feedback.

(19)

THE JOB OF THE CEO

Early on in your startup, when it's just you or you and your cofounders, you're doing all or most of the work, out of necessity. This may include research, product design, engineering, marketing, sales, customer support, and dozens of other necessary tasks. However, as your company grows—either through customer traction with your product or from recruiting new team members who believe in your mission—your responsibilities as the head of the company will shift, and you'll need to be comfortable delegating tasks and leaving some decisions to the team that you've trusted enough to bring on board. It's important to understand this before you get to that point, as decisions made early on, such as the culture of your company, are easier to set intentionally in the beginning and very difficult to change once your company grows.

When many people think of a CEO, they think of the boss—someone who makes all the decisions within a company. In reality, CEOs of big companies make very few day-to-day decisions. Their primary functions are setting high-level strategy, recruiting and hiring executive talent, ensuring the financial health of the company, demonstrating company values and culture to employees, and serving as the public face of the company.

Mathilde Collin, the cofounder and CEO of Front App, created an informative and digestible presentation about her job as CEO, which is summarized below.

THE RESPONSIBILITIES OF THE CEO

At the highest level, the CEO has just one responsibility, which is ensuring the long-term health of the company. The health of a company can be thought of in four different dimensions; each can have a profound impact on the success of the company months or years down the line:

Financial health

This entails making sure the business has enough money. The CEO should always know how long of a runway the company has and what strategic decisions could affect how much money is in the bank. For startups that have outside investors, this responsibility includes keeping existing investors informed of the financial situation, regularly meeting with prospective investors, and raising funds at the best possible time for the company—when things are going well and you have leverage, not when you're desperate for capital.

Product leadership and strategy setting

This is about building the right things at the right time. While you may eventually have a chief product officer or others responsible for product decisions, the CEO should work with them to identify the product roadmap and high-level strategy of the company. This includes being involved and aware of market research, user research, competitive analyses, and your product roadmap. The CEO steers the vision of the company and direction of the product but empowers employees to make many of the smaller decisions about how to accomplish these objectives.

Culture upkeep

This creates the best environment to achieve company goals. It's imperative to start thinking about company culture from the very beginning of your startup, because whatever culture exists (whether intentional or not) will compound as new employees join the team. Early on, state your company values for the team, and ensure that you personally live up to them, whether in the spotlight or behind the scenes. Culture upkeep also entails creating a long-term vision that others can follow, aligning your culture with your customer, focusing on improving the employee experience, and creating a hiring process that is aligned with your company values.

Executive hiring

When hiring, CEOs find the best leaders and give them the means to succeed. This is perhaps the most important responsibility for CEOs. Finding, recruiting, and hiring the best talent for each role can be the difference between success and failure. An otherwise great CEO with subpar employees and managers will have a much more difficult time than a subpar CEO with great employees and managers. As your company grows, it's important to devote time to executive hiring and investing in the professional development of your existing leadership team, so they can grow with the company.

ROLES OF THE CEO

As the CEO, you'll wear different hats at different times for different audiences. Your message to each audience may be different, and it's important to understand the different functions that you serve.

Manager

As a manager, you are making sure your direct reports are set up for success. For the executive team that you've recruited to join your company, make sure you set goals for them and give them feedback on a regular basis. A weekly one-on-one meeting is standard, during which you should cover progress on initiatives, updates on issues, and the opportunity for the individual to raise new issues, bring up personnel concerns, or provide feedback.

The public face of the company

People will want to talk to the CEO. As the CEO of a startup, you can use your title and position to write blog posts, to speak on panels or at events, and to reach out for public relations efforts. These all help with customer acquisition. The more opportunities you have to get in front of people, the more likely customers are to know about your company and product. As your company grows, you will also be contacted by journalists and others writing stories about your company, which could be positive or negative. It's important to have a measured approach when responding to requests for quotes or interview requests. Be sure that your messaging to the public is intentional and positive.

Head of internal communications

As head of internal communications, you will be making sure information flows to all teams. Sometimes, it's easy to forget that not everyone knows what we know. As the CEO, you may not realize that you have knowledge that many in your company do not. It's important to intentionally relay important and relevant communications to your employees, whether through emails or regular town-hall-style meetings. People are more motivated when they understand the reasoning behind why decisions are made, rather than just "because the boss said so." As CEO, it is your job to ensure that internal communications systems and frequency are effective at keeping your employees informed.

The buck stops here

Sometimes, you'll be making tough decisions and taking responsibility. When the CEO does make decisions for the company, it is likely because it is either a big or a difficult decision that other executives disagree on. In this role, the CEO must lead in crisis management, take ownership of big decisions, and lend a hand to teams when they are short on resources.

Understanding these roles and responsibilities early on will set you up for success as your company grows and your job as CEO transforms.

CHALLENGE

Think about the values and culture you want your company to adopt and follow as it grows. Write down a list of five important values, and for each one, write down three ways you could demonstrate these values through company policies and initiatives.

For example, one of Netflix's long-standing tenets for employees has been "freedom and responsibility," which manifests in the company's five-word expense policy, which is "Act in Netflix's best interest." Whereas most companies have long, complicated expense policies about how much can be expensed for particular items under which circumstances, Netflix chose to give its employees the freedom and responsibility to make expense decisions with this simple guideline. How will you demonstrate your company's values?

BUILDING YOUR TEAM

O nce you decide to move forward with an idea, you'll want to bring other people on board to help build your company. Your initial inclination may be to let anyone who is willing to help out on your project join the team. Even in early stages, though, it's important to be intentional about who you bring on to the team and to make sure the plans, aspirations, and desires of each team member are aligned with yours. For startups, one person can affect the culture, work ethic, collaboration, and dedication of the rest of your team.

WHAT'S YOUR GOAL?

There are many reasons people start companies. Whatever your motivation, you should be open with people you're recruiting to join your team about your goals for the startup. For example, you'll want to be up-front with recruits if you see your project as a fun side hustle, but you plan on taking a traditional internship over the summer. Similarly, if you plan to work on the startup full time after graduation and expect the people who join your team to do the same, you'll want to be clear about that expectation.

Being clear about your intentions and aspirations is important, as it will determine who you bring on board to help out. Maybe you want all the help you can get and are happy to have students help out however they can. Or maybe you only want team members who will be as dedicated to the project as you are. It's more difficult to let team members go than it is to bring them on board, so be intentional about recruiting team members to ensure your expectations for the experience are aligned.

BUILDING OUT A TEAM

At the very beginning of a startup, you usually only need a handful of people to do a few jobs—mainly to do market/customer research, build an MVP, market/sell your product, and collect customer feedback. As a founder, you'll have a big part in each of these jobs, but you can also bring people on board who are fully dedicated and responsible for each of these tasks.

One of your earliest essential roles will likely be engineering. This role will be for the person or team that designs and makes your product, whether that is hardware (physical goods) or software. You'll also need someone in marketing/customer acquisition;

this person or team creates your product and company messaging and decides channels, campaigns, and tactics to get in front of customers. You'll also want someone to handle sales/business development; for products sold to other businesses, this team is directly responsible for increasing revenue through moving leads through the sales pipeline and exploring partnerships with other companies to increase distribution and revenue channels. Finally, you'll need customer support/account management. This is the person or team responsible for ensuring customers are satisfied with your product and responding to customer feedback and complaints. It's important that customer feedback is dispersed to the rest of the team, so everyone knows what customers want or are annoyed by.

As your startup grows, you'll hire additional people in each of these departments, as well as add new roles and departments such as product, finance/accounting, HR/recruiting, administrative/office manager, business affairs/legal, public relations, and potentially many other roles. While many of the tasks that these roles are responsible for can be done by other team members early on, once they no longer have the bandwidth to best fulfill their main focus, it's time to bring someone new on board.

COMPENSATION

As long as your company isn't making any money and hasn't raised capital from investors, team members should not expect to be compensated. After all, a full-time college student working part-time for an established company would most likely be classified as an intern. You should set this expectation up front, and people who decide to join your team should do so because they're excited about the project, want the experience, or want to work with you—not because they expect to make money. To ensure there are no misunderstandings, you can have team members fill out a work for hire agreement, which provides legal protections for you and the company. Of course, if you gain traction, start making significant revenue, or raise money, you'll probably need to adjust your compensation plans.

CHALLENGE

Considering what you have learned, what are the profiles of two ideal team members who could contribute the most to your startup at this stage? What specific things do you want them to accomplish in the next one to two months? What past experiences do you think would be best suited to help your company at this stage? After considering these questions, try to figure out where and how you may find people who fit this profile, and consider reaching out to them to join your team!

CONCLUSION

Congratulations! You've now received the bulk of the information, advice, and philosophy that the students who pass through The Garage accumulate. Some of them have reached escape velocity, scaled their business to be able to work on it full time and support themselves, and even raised venture capital. Many other students' projects failed at The Garage, as most startups do, but they don't regret trying. They're now armed with knowledge and confidence for their next endeavor.

It has been one of our greatest joys to help students embrace entrepreneurship and the lessons it teaches. Students leave The Garage with confidence, boldness, and autonomy. We couldn't be prouder of our alums and the paths they are forging as innovation workers and entrepreneurs. We hope this book inspires you to do the same.

YOUR FIRST RODEO
WON'T BE YOUR LAST

We can't emphasize enough that even if the idea you're working on fails, the experience will pay dividends in the future. With each rep, you'll get smarter and faster. If you see a great opportunity, you'll be ready to seize it.

Sarah Ahmad started college as a chemical engineering major. She spent the summer between her sophomore and junior years literally watching the paint dry at an internship in the research and development department of a paint company. The following summer, Sarah had to decide between an internship at Whirlpool and working on her own idea for a startup. After seeking advice from many mentors, she took the plunge into being a full-time founder. This decision would change the trajectory of Sarah's life.

Sarah recruited a team and got to work. Her startup, HotPlate, an app for finding the best dishes at local restaurants, had amassed more than 500 users by the end of the summer. She loved working on her startup and wanted to work on it full time after graduation. Despite diligently working on HotPlate throughout her senior year, she didn't have enough user growth nor a clear monetization plan to work on her startup full time. At the end of her senior year, she decided to move on.

After graduation, Sarah took a job with a healthcare startup in Silicon Valley. She continued to mull over new startup ideas with her friend and future cofounder, Collin Pham, who had also been a student founder in college. A year later, Sarah and Collin both quit their jobs to start Mistro, a remote work benefits startup, and were accepted into Y Combinator.

They locked in some early customers for Mistro but were struggling to reach product–market fit. In the true nature of thinking like scientists, they decided to test a different solution to a different problem they were hearing about from the remote teams and startups who were their initial customers, including the other startups in their Y Combinator batch. Many of these teams did not have a physical office, worked remotely, or moved around often. This was problematic, since as a business, you must have a physical mailing address. Changing this address with all of the relevant entities is a bureaucratic and logistical nightmare.

Sarah and Collin quickly built an MVP landing page for a product that would provide a virtual mailing address for businesses to use on important documents, such as tax forms, and called it Stable. Stable took off with customers, showing much greater adoption and traction than the team had with Mistro, so they pivoted the business to focus solely on the new product.

Sarah's story exemplifies that the lessons you learn as a student founder will carry into your professional life after college. Your entrepreneurial mindset will make you a great addition to any startup team or any company that values innovation. When and if you see a problem that you want to solve, you'll have the skill set to evaluate, test, and build the idea.

Sarah offered this valuable advice: "If you know you want to be an entrepreneur someday, flex that muscle—whether it's during the evenings and weekends while working full time or keeping your networks intact as you navigate new ideas—keep hustling, follow your passion, curiosity, and intuition, and always take the path you are more excited about."

YOU CAN'T DO IT ALONE

No matter what your idea, project, venture, or startup is, you will need other people to help you, cheer you on, join you, and ultimately believe in what you're building. It can be a scary concept that you will have to rely on other people to succeed and that you can't do it by yourself in secret. But this should also be an inspiring rallying cry to ask for help, tell everyone what you're working on, and work on solving problems that you believe in.

On another level, realize there will be people who donate their time, expertise, knowledge, opinions, feedback, and input to help you succeed. Whether it's your best friend, a professor, a user giving feedback, or a potential investor that you pitched, it's unlikely they needed to take the time to share their thoughts with you. All of this input will make it more likely that you're ultimately successful.

Even outside of direct support of your idea, your family, friends, and colleagues are likely supporting you both indirectly and directly—whether volunteering to test your product out or being understanding about why you can't spend as much time with them at the moment.

Building anything worthwhile requires the support and excitement of other people. We hope that, from reading this book, you have a better idea of whom to reach out to and whom to recruit to join and support your team.

HAVE GRATITUDE

Since it will take others to help you succeed, remember to show appreciation and gratitude every step of the way. Say thank you when someone donates their time to talk with you about your idea. Be appreciative of classmates who will help get your idea off the ground without getting paid. If you win a cash award, thank the donors and organizers who made that experience possible.

Whether your venture succeeds or fails, we encourage you to look for opportunities to pay it forward to other first-time founders. What you learn along the way is invaluable to those a few steps behind you. You can pay it forward with your time, your advice, your expertise, or your money. Consider volunteering to lead or start an entrepreneurship club. Hold office hours for other students at your school's entrepreneurship center. Volunteer to speak on a panel at a local high school or event for younger founders.

If you are one of the lucky ones and you make money from your venture, consider making a financial investment in other founders. This could be in the form of a grant gifted to your school or entrepreneurship organization, or this could be in the form of an investment stake in a student-founded business.

You'll notice that throughout this book, we make very few guarantees. We don't promise a sure path to success, extreme wealth, or happiness. But if there is one thing we could guarantee, it's that if you follow the philosophy and advice in this book, it is highly unlikely that you'll ultimately regret your entrepreneurial journey.

Although it is true that the vast majority of startups eventually fail, we hope that you've seen through some of the stories that we've shared that the experience, knowledge, relationships, and stories gained through practicing entrepreneurship are more powerful than any other job or experience you could have. You'll never see the world in the same light, and you'll always be looking for the next opportunity to help others solve a problem and make your own dent in the world.

We hope you use your newly developed entrepreneurial mindset and skill set superpower for good in the world. There is no shortage of difficult problems in need of solutions. Now, more than ever, we need leaders who are innovative, adaptable, and thrive in ambiguity—in summary, those who can think and act like entrepreneurs.

IT'S TIME TO GET STARTED

You now have all the information you need to get started. Now is the time to become a *doer*, someone who doesn't just have ideas but makes them reality. You can, of course, return to this book whenever you need some guidance or inspiration (part I) or more tactical details (part II).

Our only ask of you is that if you found this book helpful and inspiring, let us know! Or if there's something you disagree with or wanted more information about, let us know that, too! We live by the principles in this book and are keen to get feedback from our customers—you. We especially enjoy hearing personal stories about the projects you're working on and how you put these concepts into practice. You can email us at authors@foundedbook.com.

Thank you for purchasing and reading our book. We hope it helps you along your journey. Good luck!

—Melissa and Mike

ACKNOWLEDGMENTS

We are so grateful to everyone who helped bring this book to life! Most importantly, we are grateful to our students for inspiring us and giving us the motivation to write our first book. We are also grateful to the current and former team at The Garage for making it a transformational place for our students: Elisa Mitchell, Elisabeth Wright, Jessa Fuller, Ben Williams, and Hayes Ferguson. We are also grateful for the countless mentors, experts, and donors who have given their time and money to support The Garage.

Thank you to our current and former students who read our manuscript and gave us their unfiltered, honest feedback and to the students and alums who shared their stories throughout the book: Lucas Philips, Mateo Price, Lainey Dow, Jihad Esmail, Katie Hoffman, Matt Zients, Charlotte Oxnam, Spencer Levitt, Austin Pager, Lauren Washington, Ibraheem Alinur, Rachel Cantor, Lucas Pasch, Akshat Thirani, Sarah Ahmad, Daniel Green, Marianne Zapata, and Sam Kim Jr.

We had no idea how to write a book, and we gained enormous insights from authors and book experts, including Roberta Rubin, Aaron Levy, Chris Steiner, and Kunal Mehta. We also appreciated the legal insights from Patrick Richards and Scott Schonfeld, who both have a talent for making complex legal issues straightforward and easy to understand.

We would also like to thank our families for their love and support. And finally, we want to thank you, our reader, for taking the time to read our book.

GLOSSARY

Every industry has its own language, jargon, and nomenclature. This can create feelings of exclusion and intimidation for those who are not familiar with them. We've brainstormed some of the most common words, acronyms, and phrases in the world of entrepreneurship and defined them here in everyday language. Some of the words are in the book, and others are not.

Accelerator: A program for helping a startup grow or accelerate from point A to point B. Accelerators help startups build out their business model and company. Like an incubator, an accelerator usually includes some combination of education, mentorship, and funding.

Advisor: A person who provides business and/or industry advice to a startup or startup founder. Sometimes advisors are volunteers, and sometimes they are compensated with money or equity in the startup.

Angel investor: A wealthy person who gives you money in exchange for equity in a startup. Angel investors usually invest very early in a startup before venture capitalists or other more "professional" investors step in.

B2B: Short for *business-to-business*. Selling a product or service from a business to another business (i.e., Salesforce).

B2C: Short for *business-to-consumer*. Selling a product or service from a business to a consumer (i.e., Chipotle).

Cap table: Short for *capitalization table*. A spreadsheet that shows all the people or businesses that own equity in a startup and what percentage each entity owns.

Churn: The percentage of customers or users who stop using your product in a subsequent time period.

Customer: The person or business that pays for your product or service (see **User**).

DAU: Daily active users. The number of people who use your website, app, or digital service each day.

Exit: An event that enables equity holders (founders, employees, investors, etc.) to achieve liquidity, typically through being acquired by another company or listing on a public market through an initial public offering.

Friends and family round: When close personal connections (friends, family, colleagues, professors) invest their own money in a startup in exchange for equity. These people usually invest because they want to support the founder even though they might not know a lot about the industry, technology, and so on.

Growth hacking: Also known as *growth marketing*, it's a marketing tactic to help grow a startup's user or customer base using conventional and unconventional digital marketing experiments and techniques.

Incubator: A program for nurturing startups that usually includes some combination of education, mentorship, and funding. Many incubators include a physical component, such as a shared workspace.

IP (intellectual property): A legal term referring to the ownership of an idea, design, or invention by the person who came up with it.

IPO: Initial public offering.

Lean startup: A methodology for building startups memorialized in a book/blog by entrepreneur Eric Ries.

Moat: Something defensible that protects what you've built from competitors, such as a key strategic partnership or market share.

Mock-up: A prototype, usually refers to a digital prototype like a wireframe of a website or app.

MVP: Minimum viable product.

NDA: Nondisclosure agreement.

OKRs: Objectives and key results.

Patents: A patent gives the creator of an idea or invention the legal right to exclude others from using it.

Pitch deck: A brief presentation (usually PowerPoint or Keynote) used to provide an overview of your startup.

Pivot: When a startup changes their customer, industry, or technology based on feedback.

Postmortem: A meeting or written piece analyzing why a startup or product failed.

Product–market fit: When what you've built meets a clear user/customer need. This is required before scaling a company.

Scope creep: A negative term for when a project's goals change or continue to grow, usually straying from the initial goals.

Stealth mode: When a startup is operating secretly, usually to avoid a competitor or before they are ready to publicly share what they are working on.

Trademark: A type of intellectual property consisting of a recognizable sign, design, or expression that identifies products or a service, like the Nike swoosh.

UGC: User-generated content. Images, video, text, and/or audio that has been posted by people (i.e., a user) to an online platform (e.g., a Yelp review).

User: The person, business, or entity that uses your product or service. Sometimes the user is also the customer.

Venture capital: A type of investment that provides money to startups with high growth potential in exchange for equity.

Viral loops: A product or marketing mechanism for driving continuous referrals to your product or service; for example, when you invite your friends to a new social network or app, that's a viral loop.

ABOUT THE AUTHORS

Melissa Kaufman

As founding executive director of The Garage, Melissa leads the team and is responsible for the overall vision for the space, programs, and community. She brings a decade of experience working for consumer technology companies in Silicon Valley. The culture at The Garage is an aggregation of her professional experiences at Google, YouTube, and consumer startups. Her entrepreneurial spirit runs deep and inspired her to found her own influencer marketing agency. Today, she helps others fulfill their entrepreneurial dreams. Melissa received her BA in computer science from Dartmouth College. This is her first book.

Mike Raab

As the associate director of The Garage, Mike's mission is to give students the resources, space, and confidence to chase their ambitions without the fear of failure and to empower them to live authentically and do work that is interesting and fulfilling to them.

His unique career has included working in the entertainment industry in Hollywood, taking a brief sabbatical to backpack through Europe for a summer, investing in and working with early-stage startups in San Francisco through Sinai Ventures, and now empowering and supporting student entrepreneurs at The Garage.

In his free time, Mike enjoys writing about technology, startups, and media. His writing has been read by hundreds of thousands of readers and published in Business Insider, OneZero, and HackerNoon, among others.

Follow Mike on Twitter at **@hithereimmike.**